DREAMS AS GOD'S LOVE LANGUAGE

A Biblical Guide to Embracing And Interpreting Your Dreams

OTI LONGE

DEDICATION

To my Lord and Savior, Jesus Christ, who set me on
this incredible journey and has been so faithful.

To my darling wife, Esther Longe, who has been an
incredible rock of support. I love and appreciate you.

To my wonderful children, Isabelle and Isaac,
Daddy loves you both dearly!

Joseph's parents and siblings did not need anyone to interpret Joseph's dream about the sun, moon, and stars bowing to him. Everyone instinctively understood the dream. Fast forward a couple centuries to the era of Daniel where no one could interpret a king's dream, *except for one man.*

The difference between these two eras is the "dream culture".

I only know a few people who have worked really hard at the grassroots level, seeking to restore dream culture and make it main stream again. Oti Longe is one of such people. His new book, *Dreams As God's Love Language*, seeks to do just that. It introduces God's people to one of the purest ways He speaks to His people without any filters.

You will be blessed by how the book equips you in the basics of dream interpretation and how to convey the redemptive purpose of dreams. If you want to be influential in the marketplace with a niche skill, read the book.

Udy Ntia

Have you ever felt the weight of a dream linger long after waking, as if it held a message too significant to ignore? Even worse are those times when you almost forget the content of the dream immediately you wake up.

In the spiritual realm, your dreams are a gate where you engage with spiritual intelligence, empowering you for the commitments God has placed upon you. Yet, it's not just about having profound dreams; it is about understanding what God is revealing to you. Oti Longe achieves precisely this in 'Dreams as God's Love Language.'

This book is more than a mere guide; it's a roadmap for those seeking to discern and interpret the messages encoded within their dreams. Whether you're a seasoned dreamer seeking interpretation, or you've been wondering why you don't dream, or you're just seeking to learn how to hear from God through dreams, Oti simplifies the language of dreams, drawing from his deep well of spiritual insight.

What sets 'Dreams as God's Love Language' apart is its relevance to the current move of God. Oti captures not only the essence of dreams but also how to maximize them for accurate alignment with God's agenda in this season of swift divine activity. The book is a timely resource, equipping readers to be attuned to God's voice in a time where such sensitivity is paramount. Importantly, it goes beyond interpretation; it is about connection.

Oti delves into why God speaks to us through dreams and how we can turn these moments into deep, personal encounters with Him, applying the lessons to our everyday lives.

So, consider this your personal invitation—dive into the pages of 'Dreams as God's Love Language' and unveil the treasures your dreams have been hiding.

Apostle Isi Igenegba

ACKNOWLEDGEMENTS

I am a man helped by God, and I sincerely want to thank and appreciate all the wonderful men and women of God that have helped me on my journey. Thank you so much for all your love and support.

I am profoundly grateful to my parents, Mr. and Mrs. Bernard Longe, for your unwavering love and support in more ways than I can mention. I also want to especially thank you for living a life of integrity that is truly worthy of emulation.

To Your Royal Majesties, Ogiame Atuwatse III and Olori Atuwatse III, thank you so much for all your love and unwavering support through the years. You have truly been family to me, and I am truly grateful.

Thank you so much, Apostle Obii Pax-Harry, for your love, timely words of counsel, and encouragement. I really appreciate you for modeling vulnerable leadership and integrity so effortlessly.

To Pastor Emmanuel and Mrs. Yinyinade Dania, thank you for being family to us and for your help and support over the years. Thank you for always giving a listening ear and for all the wise words of counsel. I am truly grateful.

To Apostle Udy and Mrs. Emo Ntia, thank you so much for your tremendous help with the birth of the promise. You effortlessly model simplicity and excellence in both the marketplace and in ministry.

Thank you so much, Apostle Isi Igenegba, for believing in me and giving me a platform to express the gifts and graces that God has bestowed. My family and I highly value and cherish you.

Thank you so much, Mrs. Ijeoma Okolie, for coming on this book-writing journey with me and for all the insights and encouragement shared. I really appreciate it.

Finally, I am incredibly grateful for the unwavering love and support of Pastor Alex Ajakaiye, who allowed himself to be used as a vessel of help for me. Your contribution to my journey cannot be understated, and I want you to know that I honor and appreciate you, sir, for everything.

FOREWORD

I am particularly excited about this book by the highly gifted, anointed, noble, and honorable prophet to the nations, Oti Longe, who has consistently pursued his passion to see an often misunderstood lineage of the prophetic ministry received in its potent nature and purpose as a tool for accomplishing the missional mandate of the church.

What makes this book a 'must read' is Oti's unique, bold yet easy-to-follow writing style. He brings a fresh and unique approach to the subject matter while sticking to the assignment of conveying the message of dreams, vision, dreaming, and interpretation succinctly. Another commendable aspect of the book lies in the expansive exegesis of the prophetic gift in operation, the ministry that flows out of the gift when in demonstration, and ultimately, its power not lying with man but in God, whose heart revealed in his word (scripture) has to be the residence of all attempts to understand dreams. The power of interpreting dreams lies with God. Oti makes this truth amply clear through the pages of this timely book, which is to be received as a work tool and a gift to the ekklesia for such a time as this.

All seers are prophets, but not all prophets are seers. The emphasis on the seer dimension of the prophetic ministry being championed through this important book is to introduce believers who primarily receive messages from the Lord through the visual (prophetic pictures) revelatory realm to embrace God's chosen way to communicate with them and to pay the price of developing their spiritual gift.

Oti painstakingly, through documented dreams, highlighted key principles of effective ministry in the exercise of the gift of prophecy. The importance of journaling, living a life of dedication to God, personal governance, etiquette, and protocols of the prophetic ministry are eternal laws that guarantee success in the use of the gift of prophecy in spiritual relationship circles and as a tool for evangelism in the marketplace and workplace. This ultimately is the heart of the father, "that none shall perish."

DREAMS AS GOD'S LOVE LANGUAGE distinguishes the fivefold ascension function of the prophet, who is primarily an equipper, and the believer - ekklesia, as those to be equipped to fulfil the new creation mandate to win souls and to change culture. This distinction empowers readers to embrace their gift in faith and to exercise same by faith for kingdom expansion. This book contains a rich bouquet of sound doctrine and revelation in harmony.

Lastly, one cannot endorse the book without inviting readers into the inner chambers of the anointed, deeply spiritual, simply amazing, disciplined, detailed, resilient, humble, thorough, and every other adjective that describes a man in whom God is well pleased. Oti Longe is an apostolic and prophetic leader to generations. He has presented a book that is a lamp and a lamp stand, a first of its kind, out of a nation of over two hundred million people, of whom over fifty percent are Christians. A thorough guide to dreams, interpretation, and the path to achieving divine purpose has emerged from a country (Nigeria), which Sue Mitchell, one of my earliest mentors, once described as a "Joseph Nation."

I highly recommend DREAMS AS GOD'S LOVE LANGUAGE, not just as another book on dreams but as a tool for daily supernatural living. It has been my pleasure to endorse a man I am privileged to know and serve and his ground-breaking book.

Obii Pax-Harry

Apostolic Leader, author, church planter, social advocate, instructor, entrepreneur, wife, mother, and grandmother.

Table of Contents

INTRODUCTION

I am a dreamer and my dreams have been one of the primary ways God speaks to me.

I started dreaming and recollecting my dreams in April 2012. Before that time, if I had been asked about dreaming, I would have said that I do not have dreams.

As a young boy, I had a dream in which I found myself in a bathroom, using the toilet. However, in reality, using the toilet in the dream coincided with me wetting my bed. Apart from that particular experience, I cannot recall ever having dreams. This changed in April 2012, which also happened to be the same period I began praying in tongues.

At first, I did not think to write my dreams down, so I would wake up, go about my day, and simply keep it moving. However, with time, it became clear to me that I was not dreaming "ordinary" dreams. They actually contained "hidden" messages for me, and I needed to know what they meant.

The first dream that stood out to me was one where I was walking through a green field with a friend. We got to a tree, and my friend climbed up the tree while I looked from below. Once she got to the top of the tree, she became fat. Then, all of a sudden, she fell to the ground, and as soon as she hit the ground, she became extremely thin. A frail-looking elderly woman approached her and engaged in conversation before eventually walking away together. I followed behind them, carefully observing their actions, until I suddenly woke up.

When I woke up from this dream, I did not understand what it meant, but the imagery stood out to me. I definitely knew that becoming fat at the top and suddenly becoming slim upon hitting the ground had a meaning, and I was curious to find out what it meant.

In my search for answers, I came across *Communion with God Ministries by Mark Vickler*. The first thing I noticed was the consistency of the advice to journal one's experiences with God, which in my case was to record my dreams. So, I started writing them down. Once I began to write down my dreams, I noticed that they occurred more frequently and were much easier to recall.

Learning Point: Taking the time to write down your dreams when you wake up is a crucial first step on the path to interpreting them.

God introduced Pastor Alex Ajakaiye into my life before I began recollecting my dreams. He is incredibly patient and empathetic, and he played a significant role in guiding me through the early years of my Christian journey. At that time, I was unaware that he had the ability to interpret dreams, since we had not previously discussed it. However, during one of our conversations, I mentioned that I had a dream that I believed was significant. He asked me to share the details of the dream with him. We prayed together, and he gave me the interpretation of the dream, which seemed good to me, and I soon shared another dream with him. Once I became aware of his ability to accurately interpret dreams, I was sufficiently happy to present my dreams to him and trust God to give me the interpretations through him.

Initially, this arrangement seemed to be effective. Despite his limited availability, he managed to interpret a few of my dreams, which provided me with a certain level of satisfaction.

~*God allowed this arrangement to work for a season*~

In the passage of time, the frequency of my dreams (sometimes up to four dreams a night for multiple nights), coupled with my mentor's unavailability, meant that I soon had a pile of dreams that I could not fully understand but knew had great meaning.

Meanwhile, inside of me was a burning hunger and a desire to know what my Father was saying!

This intense desire compelled me to pray, search, study, read, watch, and learn about dreams and the dream interpretative process. I immersed myself in the world of biblical dream interpretation, and I soon came across John Paul Jackson's teachings, videos, and books, which played a significant role in my journey to understanding and interpreting dreams from a biblical perspective.

Through my journey, I have learned valuable lessons from God, and my purpose for writing this book is to share these insights with you.

A BIBLICAL BASIS FOR UNDERSTANDING DREAMS

I have encountered a diverse range of perspectives regarding dreams and their authenticity as a legitimate means through which God communicates with people.

Some people believe that it was an "Old Testament thing" that lost its relevance following the inception of the New Testament. Some others have been trained to view dreams primarily as a channel for demonic activity, hence a fearful reaction to almost any dream. Then we have others who do not pay any mind to their dreams because they are often symbolic and do not make sense at first glance. My goal in writing this book is to give you a biblically grounded understanding of dreams, enabling you to recognize that God's love for you is on display through the dreams you receive. I also aim to help you completely overcome any inclination to embrace fear in connection with dreams and instead develop confidence in a God who longs to speak to you, including through the dreams you dream.

CHAPTER 1

Spiritual Eyes That See

There is a popular perspective about Jesus' encounter with the blind man of Bethsaida that emphasizes the fact that Jesus had to pray twice before the man was healed, thus serving as an indication for us not to give up in the place of prayer.

However, there is more to this encounter. Let's take a look:

The Blind Man of Bethsaida

Mark 8:23-25:

23 So He took the blind man by the hand and led him out of the town. And when He had spit on his eyes and put His hands on him, He asked him if he saw anything. 24 And he looked up and said, "I see men like trees, walking." 25 Then He put His hands on his eyes again and made him look up. And he was restored and saw everyone clearly.

In order to understand what really took place in this exchange between Jesus and the blind man, we need to look at Daniel's interpretation of King Nebuchadnezzar's second dream, written in Daniel 4:10-17.

After listening to the dream, Daniel pondered on it before responding with an interpretation. From his interpretation, we gain an interesting insight into one of the symbolic meanings of a tree in a dream.

Mark 8:23-25 (NKJV)	Daniel 4:13-22 (NKJV)
A Blind Man Healed at Bethsaida	Daniels Interprets King Nebuchadnezzar's Dream
23. *So he took the blind man by the hand and led him out of the town. And when He had spit on his eyes and put His hands on him, He asked him if he saw anything.*	20. **"The tree that you saw,** *which grew and became strong, whose height reached to the heavens and which could be seen by all the earth,*
24. *And he looked up and said, "**I see men like trees, walking."**	21. *Whose leaves were lovely and its fruit abundant, in which was food for all, under which the beasts of the field dwelt, and in whose branches the birds of the heaven had their home.*
25. *Then He put His hands on his eyes again and made him look up. And he was restored and saw everyone clearly.*	22. **It is you, O king**, *who have grown and become strong; for your greatness has grown and reaches to the heavens, and your dominion to the end of the earth.*

According to Daniel's interpretation, **the tree** in King Nebuchadnezzar's dream symbolized **the King** himself.

This dream illustrates how a tree can symbolize a person in a dream.

Now, when we consider Jesus' interaction with the blind man at Bethsaida, we see that it was the blind man's "spiritual eyes" that opened first, and as a result, he had the ability to see people, albeit symbolically as trees.

His natural eyesight was subsequently restored when Jesus prayed for him the second time.

In Matthew 13:13, Jesus said, *"Therefore I speak to them in parables, because seeing they do not see, and hearing they do not hear, nor do they understand."*

It is important to note that Jesus was not talking about physical blindness or deafness. Rather, He was referring to spiritual blindness and the inability to obey what one hears, which stem from having a stony heart.

In essence, we all have spiritual eyes, and it is with these eyes that we are able to receive the things we see in our dreams and have spiritual experiences.

CHAPTER 2

Sources of Dreams

Dreams from God: Conversations with Our Father

Numbers 12:6

If there were prophets among you, I, the Lord, would reveal myself in visions. I would speak to them in dreams.

Acts 2:17

And it shall come to pass in the last day, says God, that I will pour out of My Spirit on all flesh; your sons and your daughters shall prophesy, your young men shall see visions, your old men shall dream dreams.

The Bible is replete with examples of people who received dreams from God, like Abraham, Joseph, Laban, Jacob, and Daniel. There are also numerous examples of "unbelievers" in scripture who also received dreams from God, such as Abimelech, Pharaoh, and Nebuchadnezzar.

God speaks to all through dreams—both believers and unbelievers. The key question, however, is how to know if a dream is from God. The answer to this question is not as straightforward or academic as some people make it out to be.

Think about it

How can you prove that it was God who spoke to you?

The truth is, we often cannot prove that it was God who spoke to us based on the way we receive instructions. God's voice has to be discerned. The proof is oftentimes embedded in the resultant good that comes from our obedience to His instructions. As we grow in intimacy with God, our ability to discern His voice and promptings becomes sharper and much easier.

Likewise, with dreams, there is no formula.

The problem with formulas is that they inadvertently attempt to put God in a box, which is not possible.

There are several principles that can give a hint that the dream is from God. Some could be dreams filled with bright colors, some could be dreams that convey a general sense of peace and progress, some could be dreams that contain a subject matter that was not even on the dreamer's mind, and so much more. In fact, God could speak through dreams that have no color, and He can also give us dreams whose content scares us.

It is important to realize that dreams from God do not necessarily make the dreamer feel good.

Pharaoh had two dreams from God that troubled him so much that he requested the insight of all the magicians in Egypt to attempt to interpret his dream. This level of desperation proves that Pharaoh was indeed greatly troubled.

Genesis 41:8

*Now it came to pass in the morning that **his spirit was troubled**, and he sent and called for all the magicians of Egypt and all its wise men. And Pharaoh told them his dreams, but there was no one who could interpret them for Pharaoh.*

Psalm 105:16-22 gives us a fascinating behind-the-scenes look into the origins of the events that took place in Egypt and God's part in them.

16. *Moreover He called for a famine in the land; He destroyed all the provision of bread.*
17. *He sent a man before them—Joseph—who was sold as a slave*
18. *They hurt his feet with fetters, He was laid in irons.*
19. *Until the time that his word came to pass, the word of the LORD tested him.*
20. *The king sent and released him, The ruler of the people let him go free.*
21. *He made him lord of his house, And ruler of all his possessions,*
22. *To bind his princes at his pleasure, And teach his elders wisdom.*

We see that God orchestrated the famine in Egypt, which was depicted in Pharaoh's dream, and also orchestrated Joseph's elevation through his interpretation of the dream given to Pharaoh.

Someone once shared a dream with me where he saw himself going to pick up vomit from the floor to put back into his mouth. As he scooped the vomit into his hands, he woke up. The person was extremely troubled by this dream and initially believed that it had to be the work of the enemy.

It is very easy to assume that this kind of dream is a machination of the devil, and what most people tend to do is immediately declare a 21-day dry fast against all "enemies". Meanwhile, this was a correction dream from God, aimed at helping the dreamer understand what his rebellious actions looked like from God's perspective.

While pondering the dream, The Holy Spirit gave me this scripture to help me understand what the dream was about.

Proverbs 26:11

As a dog returns to its vomit, so fools repeat their folly.

The aim of the dream was to help the dreamer recognize the folly of his ways by using his return to vomit as a symbolic representation of the sin that he had been delivered and set free from, which he had begun to embrace again.

Another mistake people tend to make when judging the legitimacy of a dream and its source is to presuppose that any dream that appears to contain cartoonish elements or does not have a serious tone must not be from God.

Someone shared a dream with me that further elaborates on this principle. He said, "I once had a dream where I saw a book and a pencil on a table in front of me. I picked up the pencil and drew a short line on a page of the book. The small line I drew suddenly transformed into a face and then vanished. I repeated this action several times, and each time, I saw the same thing – the line I drew transformed into different faces and the faces belonged to people that were unknown to me."

The dream looked somewhat cartoonish in nature but contained a very profound message. **The interpretation of that dream was,** "The closer he draws to The Lord, the more God will empower him to win souls to His kingdom."

In that dream, God used a "play on words." Drawing lines in the dream referred to becoming closer to God, and the faces represented souls.

The look of a dream does not necessarily convey its inherent meaning or significance. In fact, the most simple-looking actions and events in a dream may be depicting events with very weighty and far-reaching consequences.

A Dream from God is a Word from God:

In Genesis 37:6–7, 9, Joseph had two dreams that he naively—some would say foolishly—revealed to his brothers, further inciting their envy and enmity against him.

Dream 1

Genesis 37:6-7

6 So he said to them, "Please hear this dream which I have dreamed:

7 There we were, binding sheaves in the field. Then behold, my sheaf arose and also stood upright; and indeed your sheaves stood all around and bowed down to my sheaf."

Dream 2

Genesis 37:9

Then he dreamed still another dream and told it to his brothers, and said, "Look, I have dreamed another dream. And this time, the sun, the moon, and the eleven stars bowed down to me."

His dreams made his brothers hate him even more. This set off a chain of events, and thereafter, Joseph was sold into slavery, falsely accused of rape, sent into prison, and then ultimately elevated by Pharaoh to the position of Prime Minister of Egypt. While in this position in Egypt, his dream was fulfilled, and his brothers bowed down to him (Genesis 42:5–6).

Joseph spent thirteen years in Egypt as a slave and prisoner before his elevation by Pharaoh and another seven years as Prime Minister during the season of abundance before the famine, which precipitated the need for his brothers to come to Egypt in search of food.

Therefore, it took twenty years from the time of having the dreams about his prophetic destiny to the manifestation of the dreams.

In **Psalm 105:19,** we see God's perspective on Joseph's dream: *"Until the time that his word came to pass, the word of the Lord tested him."*

What was the word of The Lord to Joseph?

His dreams.

The Bible equates Joseph's dreams to a word from God to him, which tested and refined him until the season of manifestation. A dream from God is a word from God and should be treated with the seriousness and attention that you would give to any other avenue through which God speaks to you.

This brings us to the question on a lot of people's hearts: "How can I tell if my dream is from God?"

Is My Dream From God?

A number of people assert that since God is light and the Bible is replete with vivid accounts of spiritual experiences, the presence of color in a dream is typically a reliable indicator that it is a dream from God. While this may be true, dreams without any discernible color in them can also be from God.

Another widely held belief is that a dream from God, by necessity, remains etched in your memory long after you have awakened from it. While it is true that some dreams may not be forgotten after waking up, there are also dreams from God that can only be faintly remembered. If one fails to promptly record these dreams, their essence will indeed fade from their memory. This is why it is important to build the habit of diligently recording your dreams right after you wake up.

The truth is that there is no fool-proof formula for recognizing God as the source of a dream. Our walk with God will always require a level of faith and discernment to consistently recognize His voice.

People usually want a fool-proof methodology by which they can identify what is from God and what is not. I find that this level of certainty is often not provided in any endeavor with God. Just as walking with God always requires a degree of faith. This same principle applies in recognizing His voice through dreams.

One thing to note when trying to understand if a dream is from God is that **He will never violate His word;** God is His word; and He does not break His word; therefore, the accurate interpretation of a dream will never violate the word of God.

Self-Generated Dreams

Self-generated dreams refer to dreams that we cause ourselves to dream, usually as a result of the preponderance of our thoughts, emotions, and anxiety on a specific subject matter, which can eventually filter into our dreams.

Ecclesiastes 5:3 states that dreams can come when there are many cares. In another translation, it says dreams can come when there is much activity. This is why we must guard our heart with all

15

diligence, for indeed, the issues of life flow from whatever we allow to prevail in our heart.

Jeremiah 29:8 is more direct, *"For thus says the LORD of hosts, the God of Israel: Do not let your prophets and your diviners who are in your midst deceive you, nor listen to your dreams **which you cause to be dreamed**."*

It is quite common to have experiences where something you just watched shows up in one form or another in your dream, and there is a temptation to disregard it as self-generated simply because it was based on something you watched before going to bed.

In fact, God often incorporates activities and events from our waking life into our dreams in a way that should ideally make it easier for us to relate to and understand what He has been trying to say to us.

Job 33:14 lets us know that God is always speaking. The question is, are we able to recognize and discern His voice?

Intimate Relationships

Self-generated dreams are particularly common in the context of intimate relationships.

In a dating relationship, there may come a point where one person decides to end the relationship for various reasons. It is quite common for the party who still desires the relationship to start having dreams about reuniting with their ex.

Sometimes, these dreams can be relentless and begin to create a false sense of hope that the relationship will be repaired. A painful aspect of having and misinterpreting these types of recurring dreams is the mistaken belief that God is the one directing the dreamer's attention towards "the one that got away" and attempting to warn them not to let it happen.

All of these factors can combine to create false hope, often causing people to cling to dreams that they believe are from God but are actually a result of their own strong desires.

It is important for us to thoroughly examine the desires of our hearts to ensure that we are not mistakenly attributing communication to God that is actually based on our own thoughts and intentions.

Dreams from the Enemy?

This is an aspect of dreams that causes a lot of people a great deal of anxiety and confusion; when not properly understood, it can serve to limit our ability to see the great value embedded in what at first glance appears to be negative.

It is very important to establish that there is no mention in the Bible of satan being the source of any dreams.

In fact, there are several dreams in the Bible that could easily have been attributed to satan because the dreamer woke up very troubled.

Examples of these include Pharaoh's dream, Nebuchadnezzar's dream, Pontius Pilate's wife, etc.

In Job 7:14, Job attributed the source of his nightmares to God by saying, "Then You scare me with dreams and terrify me with visions."

There are indeed several schools of thought on this matter, with many people convinced that the source of nightmares and dreams that seemingly depict evil are from the devil. Upon closer examination, we will find that this is not necessarily the case.

From what perspective are you looking?

When viewed from the right perspective, dreams that appear to be depicting evil are actually giving us invaluable spiritual intelligence about the works of the enemy and the strategy the enemy is already using or plans to use against us in the future.

The question to ask yourself is, why would an enemy who is very wise and cunning reveal his intended mode of attack to his victim?

In order to see these dreams for what they are, we will need to shift our perspective to begin to see them from God's perspective.

Someone shared the dream below with me once, which serves to illustrate this point.

"In the dream, I saw myself praying in my room when, all of a sudden, the scene changed and I found myself in a dungeon. The door was opened for me by a dwarf, whom I soon realized was a witch's assistant. I boldly walked inside and saw a witch seated on a high chair. The witch came to me, and after we exchanged a few words, I began to issue prayer commands and decrees, "I bind you in the name of Jesus; I come against you in the name of Jesus." As I vehemently declared these things, the witch was seated on her high chair with her head on her hands and a look that said, "Are you done?" I could see that what I was saying had no effect on the witch. When I realized this, I tried to remember some scriptures so I could quote and use them while declaring against the witch, but I could not remember any. Several other things happened, and then the dream ended."

This dream was a source of great concern to the dreamer and as far as she was concerned, it was satan who gave her the dream. When she shared it with me, I saw it as an excellent example and demonstration of God's love for her.

The dream started off with the dreamer praying in her room before she was ushered into the confrontation with the witch. This sequence of events helps to establish the role of prayer in her ability to know. She was first praying, and then she knew. It was her time in prayer that ushered her into the insight and revelation that the dream provided.

Next, she saw a witch, and the witch confronted her. Where in times past she may have been praying "general" prayers without any real clarity on what she was up against, the dream made it clear that there was indeed a witch contending against her.

She soon began to pray fervently in the dream, making battle commands and declarations, but as she does all of these, the witch is unperturbed and makes it very clear and obvious. This helped the dreamer understand that her prayers in their current form were ineffective and had no real impact on her adversary.

The beautiful thing about the dream is that the solution was also embedded in the dream, albeit hidden and concealed, requiring discernment to recognize. The dreamer saw herself trying to remember scriptures but could not recall any for use in the place of prayer. This inability to recall any scriptures in the dream was symbolic of the Word of God missing from her heart. She may have known the scriptures and provided a mental accent by quoting them, but without the scriptures imprinted on her heart, she did not really know the revelation embedded in them.

This made it clear that the dreamer needed to meditate on the word of God, especially in the area of identity and authority. With the scriptures imprinted on her heart, her prayers would have spiritual impact because she would be praying not from head knowledge but from true conviction based on the knowledge of her authority in Christ.

Why would the devil provide all of these insights to a believer? Would he not be better served if she continued to pray ineffectively, as she had been doing in the past?

How we see and what we are looking to see are very important to our ability to recognize God's love for us, even through the seemingly negative dreams we dream.

A Dream is Not a Prerequisite for Evil to Occur

People have a tendency to erroneously treat dreams as if they are an entity that must be fought, particularly in countries that place a large emphasis on superstitions. This is why you come across statements such as, "I am praying against the dream."

These statements point to an innate propensity to suppose that a dream may be the source or origin of the problems a person is going through in their life. This can't be further from the truth!

To put it in the simplest terms possible, a dream from God is essentially God communicating with you through the medium of moving pictures. A dream is a **vehicle** through which a message is conveyed to the dreamer. Your dream is not an entity. Dreams do not cause events to occur; rather, they provide insight into events that have already happened, are still happening, or have been predetermined to happen in the future. This is a really important point to note because there is a lot of uncertainty about what a dream is and whether or not dreams have the power to produce consequences by their very nature.

Usually, as a result of the lack of clarity surrounding the nature and function of dreams, a great number of people develop a fear of dreaming because their dreams appear to portend bad occurrences in their waking lives. This should not be the case.

Think about it – evil things occur whether we dream about them or not. The dream is not the source of the "attack", it simply reveals it.

Ponder on this analogy.

An international businessman in the 16th century had various business interests in different parts of the world, and the only reliable mode of communication was through letters. He went to Mexico for a six-month sabbatical, and while he was there, he kept receiving letters from his business managers in Portugal. The letters provided updates on his business interests in Portugal.

When the businessman opened the first letter that he received from his business manager, he realized that it contained information exposing the adversarial moves of one of his business competitors who was trying to forcefully gain control of his share of the market.

Soon, the businessman received another letter, and within it was information about how his competitor had colluded with the regulators to institute regulatory action against his company. A few days later, he received yet another letter, painting a vivid picture of what would happen to his business if he did not act promptly.

Food For Thought: In this analogy, were the contents of the letters responsible for the events that took place, or did they simply serve to inform the businessman of what was going on?

Would it be wise for the businessman to start burning the letters without reading them simply because he did not like the content?

This is what some people do. They neither like nor feel good about what they see in their dreams, and as a result, they blame the dream as the source of the negative outcomes. They even begin to pray against "dreams".

Just as the letters provided invaluable information to the businessman, likewise, our dreams also provide us with priceless information. This information, when correctly interpreted, can assist us in preventing, changing, and in some cases, preparing ahead to avoid the full intended impact that would have otherwise occurred.

Did the dreams of Pharaoh produce a famine in Egypt?

If we follow the reasoning that ascribes negative outcomes to a dream, it would mean that Pharaoh's dream was responsible for the seven years of abundance and the seven years of famine. But that is not true!

Psalm 105:16-17

16. Moreover He (GOD), called for a famine in the land; He destroyed all the provision of bread. 17. He sent a man before them – Joseph, who was sold as a slave.

It is clear that it was not Pharaoh's dream that brought about the famine, but God's sovereign decision for a famine to occur. The dream simply revealed to Pharaoh something God had decided to do.

The moment you begin to look at your dreams from this perspective, what used to cause fear and apprehension will become a much cherished gift that equips you with the invaluable ability to know.

CHAPTER 3

Dreams: A Vehicle for the Revelation Gifts

Paul lists nine gifts of the Holy Spirit in 1 Corinthians 12:8–10. Of these, three are popularly referred to as the *Revelation Gifts* because of their propensity to reveal things to us. They are:

- **Word of Knowledge**: A revelation of past or current events
- **Word of Wisdom**: An insight into the mind of God concerning the future
- **Discerning of Spirits**: An insight into which spiritual entity (good or evil) is governing a given situation

These three gifts manifest through different "vehicles". For instance, some people have a sudden knowing from impressions laid on their hearts; some can hear audibly; while others receive revelations through visions, dreams, and trances.

Dreams from God often contain at least one of the revelation gifts in operation, while at other times there is a combination of different gifts in manifestation during the same dream. These help to provide valuable insight to the dreamer, including helping to unravel seemingly impossible situations. A lot of times, God answers our prayers by revealing to us the real cause of our experience.

The "real" reason for a lot of the situations that occur in people's lives is usually much different than they think, hence the need for revelation in order to effectively understand and accurately begin to deal with them.

The Word of Knowledge

The Wise Men Warned In a Dream: Matthew 2:12

When Jesus was born, the wise men saw His star and sought to worship Him. The news of their search got to Herod, and he requested to meet with them. In the process, he got significant information from them about when they initially saw the star.

Herod encouraged them to locate Jesus and bring word back to him ostensibly so he could also go and pay homage to the child, even though his real motive was to destroy the child. After the wise men worshipped Jesus and gave Him gifts, they had a dream where God warned them not to return to Herod.

This dream was a word of knowledge from God to them because it revealed to them Herod's true motive, which they were seemingly unaware of.

The Word of Wisdom

King Nebuchadnezzar Judged: Daniel 4:9-34

King Nebuchadnezzar had a dream in which he received judgment from God. Daniel interpreted his dream to mean that his kingdom was going to be taken from him for a season until the king acknowledged the supremacy of The Almighty God in his heart.

While it took a *whole year* for the judgment to be executed, from the very moment the words were uttered in the realm of the spirit, King Nebuchadnezzar's fate was sealed.

From this example, we see that the source (God) of his judgment was revealed to the king, and a future event was also revealed in the same dream.

Discerning Of Spirits

There is a spiritual world that is more real than the physical world, which we see with our eyes. The spiritual world takes precedence over the natural world and is, in fact, the main domain where decisions are taken and implemented.

> **Key Point**: Before anything takes place on earth, it has first been established in the realm of the spirit. Through the revelation gifts, God empowers us to know. We have an insightful encounter recorded in Acts 16, where Paul and his companions attracted the attention of a slave girl who followed them everywhere and continuously proclaimed, "These men are the servants of the Most High God, who proclaim to us the way of salvation." She did this for several days until Paul was fed up with her antics and decided to cast out the spirit that was motivating her actions.

This situation provides an interesting insight into the importance of accurately discerning the spirit at work in a situation.

At face value, the slave girl was correct in her assertion that Paul and Silas were servants of the Most High God who had come to proclaim the way of salvation. However, she knew the truth and proclaimed it through the influence of a spirit of divination.

She was saying the right thing, but the source of what she was saying was evil.

Through the gift of discerning of spirits, Paul was not fooled by the accuracy of her assertion. He was able to discern that it was not The Holy Spirit motivating her utterance.

Therein lies another principle to take note of. Whatever you cannot identify, you cannot exercise spiritual authority over.

Acts 6:18

*18. And this she did for many days. But Paul, greatly annoyed, turned and **said to the spirit**, "I command you in the name of Jesus Christ to come out of her." And he came out that very hour.*

The scripture above shows that when Paul decided to address the situation, he spoke directly to the spirit at work in her. Once identified, Paul could easily exercise authority over it and command it to leave.

The devil loves to keep his involvement in a matter as veiled as possible, thereby causing the person experiencing the negative effects of his involvement to be confused about the real source of whatever challenge they may be going through.

Through dreams, God reveals the truth to help us know what we are really dealing with and how to overcome it.

A dream shared with me some time ago perfectly illustrates this. In the dream, the dreamer found herself in a house with her mother and two of her sisters. There was a huge crocodile in the house, which stood in front of the restroom like it was standing guard to prevent anyone from going in there. Everyone else seemed okay and unperturbed by the presence of the crocodile, except the dreamer. The crocodile moved around the house freely but always went back to the door of the restroom, closely guarding it. Then she woke up.

26

In the dreamer's family, both her parents are still married, and they have four girls; however, in her dream, only her mother, her two siblings, and herself were present in the house.

This is the starting point for understanding what the dream refers to. I asked her about the similarities that exist among the people in the dream that were absent in the other two that were not in the dream.

From her response, it became easier to discern what the dream was about and why a crocodile was used to depict the problem.

The people in the dream had a tendency to communicate in a way that was direct but could sometimes be seen as abrasive and unwittingly hurtful. On the other hand, her father and other sister did not have that tendency. They were both soft-spoken and tend to be more considerate in the way they express themselves.

A crocodile is a prehistoric-looking animal that can symbolically represent an ancestral, familiar spirit. It has a large snout with sharp teeth and can cause excessive damage from its bite. This is a symbolic representation of the harm that the mouth can cause through hurtful and biting words.

The presence of the crocodile positioned as a guard near the restroom served as a symbol, representing a restriction on their capacity to acknowledge the necessity for repentance. This is often typified as a mindset that justifies the actions taken, regardless of how they come across.

This dream revealed the spiritual entity at work in the bloodline, its effect, and how it worked to prevent them from recognizing the issue and truly repenting of it.

CHAPTER 4

God's Love in Action: The Importance and Purpose of Dreams

God loves you, and He wants the absolute best for you.

It is essential that this truth be firmly impressed upon your heart and is the lens through which you view your interactions with Him. The bible tells us, "For God so loved the world, that He sent His only begotten Son, that whoever believes in Him may not perish but have everlasting life."

"So loved" is such a deep testament to the motivation behind His enormous sacrifice. "Whoever" means exactly what it says—whoever. It is an invitation open to all, and it is up to each individual person to accept it.

In 1 Timothy 2:2-4, we see that it is God's desire that *all men* be saved and come to the knowledge of the truth. Again, there is no restriction on His love for us.

"Whoever" and "all" are very broad terms that communicate an open-arm policy to all that will accept and embrace the offer. God has made these things freely available to us, and He is always speaking, seeking to help us recognize and make the right choices.

In **Job 33:14-18**, we see a picture of a loving Father, often trying to communicate with His children, who for different reasons are unable to accurately perceive or discern what He is really saying.

14."*For God may speak in one way or in another,* yet man does not perceive it.

15. In a dream, in a vision of the night, When deep sleep falls upon men, while slumbering on their beds.

16. Then He opens the ears of men and **seals their instruction.**

17. In order to **turn man from his deed** *and* **conceal pride** *from man.*

18. **He keeps back his soul from the pit and His life from perishing by the sword**

To summarize this passage of scripture, God often tries unsuccessfully to get through to us during the day, so He speaks to us at night when it is much easier for us to receive from Him without any distractions.

Take a minute to reflect on this.

God loves **you** so much that even when you ignore or misunderstand what He is trying to say to you during the day, He comes back at night to make sure you receive the message.

This is real love!

God does not give up on you. He is actively rooting for you.

God is love, and it is essential that we renew our minds to accurately see that every action He takes is an act of love towards us, including the dreams we receive from Him.

Common Types of Dreams

- Dreams that build faith through the power of sight

Dreams are awesome because, although we hear God in different ways, it is only through dreams, visions and trances that we get to see what He is saying.

The power of sight cannot be underestimated because once you have seen something, it cannot be unseen. The image will be etched in the heart and provides a core focus for the dreamer in the place of prayer. In fact, the man who can see is more likely to have a greater amount of faith in the place of prayer than the person who only hears about a thing.

A man once presented me with this dream:

In the dream, it was nighttime, and I was in a staff car park with lots of company and staff vehicles parked. It was a very tight space. Work ended and I had to leave, so I proceeded to my car, which was a brand new white Peugeot 504 (the old 80s model). A company driver was in charge of driving it. While attempting to come out of the car park, there was a lot of traffic from the incoming and outgoing cars. The driver tried to maneuver as best as he could, but an incoming vehicle crushed into our car from the right-hand side and then drove off without stopping. The driver and I got down to inspect the damage. The axle was twisted and the car wasn't drivable. I was distraught and kept asking God why – I was barely coping and the cost of this damage was something I could not pay.

The setting of this dream was nighttime, which is usually indicative of works of darkness being revealed to the dreamer. At the time, the dreamer was about to make an exit from his organization, and the crux of the dream was to ensure careful navigation of that exit as some contention may arise to jeopardize his ability to make the move.

A very interesting aspect of this dream was the inclusion of the Peugeot 504, which the dreamer, an IT professional, recognized as symbolic of a 504 gateway communication error.

The Peugeot 504 in itself contained a great key to understanding what the dream was about and the wisdom required to effectively navigate.

- **Correction Dreams:**

Dreams are one of the conduits through which God brings correction to His children. The beauty of dreams is that they are intrinsically private.

Hebrews 12:6-7 *"For The Lord disciplines and corrects those whom He loves and punishes every son whom He receives and welcomes [to His heart]."*

No one else gets to know your dream until you share it with them. God does not seek to embarrass us, so His correction is usually private to begin with. However, I have found that God will go to whatever lengths and costs (including your dignity) to redeem us if we continue to ignore his private correction.

Correctional dreams can sometimes be difficult to discern if we view them through the wrong lens.

For example:

John goes into a restaurant to purchase some food. He patiently waits for his turn. When he is next in line to be served, the attendant skips him and calls on the next person in the queue to place his order. This infuriates John and he has an angry outburst, yelling at the attendant while being very visibly upset and enraged. Other customers in the queue try to calm him down. The dream ends.

It is very easy and common for people to have the dream above and believe that God is showing them a fault in the life of the fast food attendant. This is even more prevalent when the dream contains people you know in real life to be antagonistic troublemakers.

The truth is that this dream is about John, and it highlights to him that there is a need to deal with his anger, temper, and inability to control his emotions even when he has been wronged. His inability to control his emotions cost him the opportunity to access what would have been nourishing to his soul. The attendant in the dream was simply a conduit through which God showed John what was in his heart.

We sometimes learn how to mask our outward emotions without dealing with the issue in our hearts. Dreams reveal the deep things of the heart and help us accurately identify issues we need to address. This is important because if an issue is not dealt with, it is only a matter of time before it manifests itself outwardly.

- **Dreams that come with instructions and directions**

Instructions embedded within dreams are very significant because they often provide solutions and guidance to seemingly impossible situations.

Recognizing the instructions in most dreams often requires a high level of discernment. These instructions are often concealed in a way that can be easily missed if one does not pay proper attention to the details of the dream.

33

In a dream I had, I was in a restaurant, sitting with three other people I did not know. A song came on the radio, and in that song, a guy was apologizing to a girl for breaking her heart. A conversation ensued between me and the lady at the table. (This dream is analyzed in full detail in the bonus chapter)

In the dream shared above, the song playing on the radio was not directed at me in any obvious way. It was simply a song that was played for all to hear. I also heard it, and when I woke up, I remembered it. Embedded in that seemingly innocuous song was a very important instruction that was eventually instrumental to my getting married.

In the earlier pages of this book, the dream shared about a witch and the dreamer, whose prayers were ineffective, contained both revelation and instruction. The instruction was, however, not obvious and needed to be discerned.

Most people are waiting for God to give them audible and direct instructions. Meanwhile, I find that, more often than not, God abides by the principle embedded in **Deuteronomy 30:19**.

19.I call heaven and earth as witnesses today against you, that I have set before you life and death, blessing and cursing; therefore, choose life, that both you and your descendants may live;

Through dreams, God presents us with options and expects us to identify and deliberately desire to walk according to His will, as depicted in His word.

- **Warning Dreams:**

A lot of dreams people generally refer to as negative dreams are actually warning dreams. They show an impending danger ahead or show the dreamer the potential outcome of their current decisions. In essence, they reveal what will happen if a deviation is not made from the dreamer's current path.

These dreams depict a negative event or occurrence. Sometimes the dreamer is shown victorious at the end of the dream, escaping the issue at hand. Other times, the dream ends abruptly with no sign of how things ended.

> **Learning Point:** A dream that depicts an event and shows victory is **an encouragement** to the dreamer that if they apply themselves to prayer and obey His leading in that area, victory is already assured. This is not a call to ignore the dream. It is an assurance that God has already given you victory before you even start acting on it.

God does this to encourage us because sometimes the situations the dream talks about will persist over an extended period of time, and the dreamer may start becoming weary and discouraged. Remembering that God has already given victory should keep the dreamer inspired to keep pressing ahead.

One of the characteristics of dreams revealing the enemy's activities is that they are usually set at night or in the dark. This is usually an indication that what you are witnessing is the **enemy's plan revealed**.

The dream shared above, about the dreamer and his Peugeot 504 *(page 29)*, was a warning dream, revealing to the dreamer, the enemy's plan to sabotage his ability to make the move by using contention.

Armed with this information, it became easier for the dreamer to by wisdom, safely navigate out of the organization. Situations arose where without prior warning, he may have reacted angrily, but because he had been warned already about how the enemy planned to cause sabotage, it was easier to regulate his emotions effectively.

Warning dreams provide us with knowledge and by wisdom, we can effectively utilize the knowledge we have received to our advantage.

CHAPTER 5

Why Does God Have Us Searching For Answers?

Why does God have us searching for answers?

This is a question in a lot of people's hearts!

Why does God not speak to me plainly? Why speak to me in parables and symbolic images when He knows I will not understand what He is trying to say?

This frustration has actually caused some people to ignore their dreams. They think to themselves, If God really wants to speak to me, He knows how to reach me. This perspective is wrong and can cause the dreamer to miss out on the invaluable information and insight God desires to share with them.

To answer the question of why, let's take a look at the book of Proverbs.

Proverbs 25:2 *It is the glory of God to conceal a matter. But the glory of kings is to search out a matter."*

From this scripture, we see that it is to God's glory (honor, majesty) to conceal certain things. God is glorified by the mysteries He keeps hidden. The scripture also says that it is the glory (honor and majesty) of kings to search out a matter.

Revelations 1:6 *He (Jesus) has made us kings and priests to His God and Father; to Him is glory and dominion forever and ever. Amen.*

In this scripture, we see that through the death and resurrection of Jesus, all born-again Christians have become kings and priests. One of the ways we manifest our kingship is to be a people who diligently search out matters.

What does it mean to search out a matter? The Hebrew word for search in this scripture is *hă·qōr,* which means to penetrate and to examine intimately.

This is not talking about a casual search that is undertaken half-heartedly. This speaks of a diligent and persistent search that must first begin with a decision in your heart. There is a certain kind of heart that seeks and searches—a *heart that places value on and honors the things of God.*

Solomon's example is a template for what the outworking of a kingly heart that searches really entails. We see in 1 Kings 3:11–15 that God blessed Solomon with wisdom. Most people assume that Solomon had no further role to play in the expression of the gift in his life. This could not be further from the truth.

Ecclesiastes 1:13 *And I set my heart to seek and search out by wisdom concerning all that is done under the heaven.* **Ecclesiastes 1:17** *And I set my heart to know wisdom and to know madness and folly.* God blessed Solomon with wisdom, but the expression of it in his life required him to diligently apply himself in pursuit of whatever he needed to understand. Likewise, we also need to set our hearts to seek and diligently search out what God has kept for us.

What you get cheaply, you hardly value. So, if you really place value on understanding what God has to say, prove it by your diligent pursuit of the matter kept concealed for your discovery.

CHAPTER 6

Stewarding Your Dreams

Record Your Dreams

Habakkuk 2:2:

"Then The LORD answered me and said:

Write the vision

And make it plain on tablets,

That he may run who reads it."

God instructed Habakkuk to write down the vision. In Revelations 1:11, Jesus Christ said to John, **"What you see, write in a book."** The first step to showing God how much you value His communication with you is to record it. By recording your dream when you wake up from it, you can have a clear and consistent recollection of the entire dream with all the pertinent information retained. I have also consistently seen that in the process of writing down my dreams, The Holy Spirit helps me to recollect parts of the dream I had forgotten or did not initially recollect.

Recording your dreams may be achieved in a variety of ways, including:

1. Writing them in a physical journal.

2. Using a voice recorder.

3. Typing them on an electronic note-taking application.

Whichever avenue is utilized in recording your dreams, it is always important to record it immediately after you wake up from the dream because, with the passage of time, our ability to accurately recollect the details in our dreams drastically diminishes.

When writing down your dream, always ensure to **include the date and any other significant events** that occurred prior to having the dream, including your prayer requests the night you had the dream.

I personally recommend keeping an electronic dream journal for two reasons:

1. It is much easier to search for any dream based on the keywords contained in it.

2. You never run out of space and can maintain the same journal, unlike physical journals with limited capacity that need to be changed periodically.

Different people have different approaches. Some wake up and pray about the dream they had before recording it, while others first record it and then pray. Whichever order you choose, they are essential.

Personally, I wake up and record the dream first, then ponder over it before praying about it. I do this because I like to write it down while I can still recall every single detail. It is also critical that my prayers are focused on the "real" issue that God is talking about.

A lot of times, people pray with a lack of understanding about what they have just been shown in the dream, which can amount to praying "amiss". One of the best ways to address this while seeking understanding is to pray in tongues. It is the Holy Spirit leading you to pray about what He has just shown you. You can't beat that!

The Holy Spirit is Involved as You Record Your Dreams

The way a dream is recorded is often integral to the interpretation of the dream. The Holy Spirit helps, as the dream is being recorded, to ensure that the integral pieces are captured accurately.

For example, when my mother's 60th birthday was coming up and there were different considerations on the best location for the birthday celebration—Nigeria or abroad—I had a dream. At the time, I was the only one of my siblings who was in Nigeria. The others were either working abroad or still in school.

An excerpt of the dream:

In the dream, I was at a place that looked somewhat like an airport, and I knew that my siblings and mom were on a flight that was scheduled to land at 6 o'clock. When the plane landed, it made a slight turn directly parallel to where I was walking, so that I could see some of the passengers on the flight and they could see me. When the passengers disembarked from the plane, my siblings and mom came to where I was standing, and we kept on walking together.

I had this dream in April, wrote it down, and pondered it, but did not understand this part of the dream. On the 31st of May, while worshipping, I suddenly received an understanding of what the dream was talking about.

On the occasion of my mom clocking 60, all my siblings were going to come to my location. God was showing me ahead of time that the celebration would take place in Lagos. The time, 6 o'clock, was a play on words for "clocking 60," and my mom's presence on the plane with them was to emphasize that this aspect of the dream was about her.

> **Learning Point**: Pay attention to people who seemingly appear randomly in your dream. God is usually showing you that the situation depicted in the dream also applies to the person who seemed to appear "randomly" in that part of the dream.

This dream serves to emphasize The Holy Spirit's help in writing dreams down because there are several ways of writing down 6 o'clock.

I could have written:

a) 6 in the evening

b) 6 am

c) 6 pm

d) 18:00

e) 6:00

By writing 6 o'clock, the interpretation of the dream was embedded in how it was written down.

As you set out to diligently honor God by recording what you receive from Him, be conscious that The Holy Spirit will partner with you in this regard.

Share as He Leads (Disobedience Has A Cost)

Dreams that seem to involve other individuals can often present a dilemma for the dreamer, particularly when it comes to deciding if to share the dream with the person it involves or to keep it to themselves. Some people share everything they see, while others decide to keep everything to themselves.

The answer actually lies somewhere in between.

Before you go ahead to share, there is a need to ensure that The Holy Spirit is leading you to do so. A lot of people have inadvertently gone ahead to plant fear in the hearts of people they shared their dreams with, either because the receiver was not able to handle it or because the person telling the dream was not able to properly convey the redemptive aspect of God's heart in whatever message was being communicated through the dream.

There are two major reasons God puts other individuals in our dreams: for intercession and for our knowledge.

- **Intercession:** God's purposes for giving us dreams about other people vary. The primary reason is that He is giving the dreamer an opportunity to partner with Him concerning the situation depicted in the dream through intercession. Our primary response should be to agree with God concerning His will for the person in your dream.

If it is a dream about elevation, progress, promotion, and more, intercede on behalf of the person to see it established in their life. In the same vein, if it is a dream depicting demotion, problems, hindrances, or similarly negative events, intercede to stop what was revealed and to establish God's will in the life of the person.

- **Knowledge**: God also gives us dreams about people to help us know. With knowledge, we are able to make more informed decisions based on the additional information available to us. This is an added benefit of developing intimacy with God, and it is essential to understand that not everything God reveals to you should be divulged.

Information provided through dreams can sometimes be concealed and easy to miss if we are not paying attention.

The Swimming Goggles Dream

Some time ago, I had a dream where I found myself surrounded by many familiar faces. As I went around greeting people, I noticed that one person I interacted with was wearing swimming goggles.

The dream was not about this individual per se, but embedded within the dream is a divinely revealed insight specifically highlighting the person's eyes and his ability to perceive spiritual matters with clarity.

Water is symbolic of the Spirit, and swimming goggles help you see clearly underwater. So the swimming goggles in this context were to reveal to me that this person has the gift of seeing clearly in the spirit. Simply speaking, he is a seer.

So, what happens when we are given the privilege of partnering with God but decide not to participate?

An abundance of revelation without a proper understanding of one's identity in Christ can lead to a skewed perspective of why you are actually receiving the revelation to begin with, and this is what happened in my situation. The revelatory insight I was receiving, coupled with a lack of understanding about the responsibility that came with it, meant that I simply viewed it as part of my "special" relationship with God. Where I should have acted, I often did not until I learned the hard way. Some examples come to mind.

A couple of years ago, I had this dream about a very senior manager at work.

Fire Incident Dream

I was on a balcony with Mr. Olumide. He appeared to have some black stains on him from smoke exposure. He said that there had been a fire. On the ground, I saw a fire truck that had been used to quench the fire. He indicated that he had to go back to either continue trying or to access the damage.

After waking up from the dream, I promptly recorded it in my dream journal. However, I didn't give it much thought until one day, three months later, the senior manager came into the office at lunchtime and headed directly towards our trading desk.

He said, "Can we believe that there was a fire at his house the night before?"

I froze at my desk, and my heart began to race. My mind immediately went to the dream I had.

He went on to describe how he was asleep when his son came into the room to wake him up because the fire alarm was on and there was a fire. He ran out and took the fire extinguisher to put out the fire. When he was able to put it off, he ran outside with his family. He noticed that the smoke did not seem to subside, and after one of his security men went back in, he also decided to jump right back into the fire as well. They eventually put out the fire, and no one was harmed.

I was so relieved that no one was harmed during the incident, but I felt guilty and wondered if God had intended for me to actually warn him ahead of time about the fire incident. I also could not help but wonder, "What if someone had died?" The remorse would have been impossible to bear.

After the incident, I moved on, and as time went by, I had another dream. This time, it was about a classmate from secondary school whom I wasn't actively in contact with at that time.

Hidden Inheritance Dream

In the dream, I entered a house and saw a woman and a man sitting down. I asked for Pascal, and she told me that he was not around. She proceeded to say that she was sure Pascal's dad left some money behind for him, but they had not found it, and Pascal was not admitting to receiving it. Then the woman and the man got down on the floor and were searching for something when Pascal walked into the room. He did not acknowledge them and walked into his own room, and I followed him in.

When I had this dream, I knew that it had something to do with his inheritance, but I did not pray about it or try to reach out to him. About five years after I had this dream, Pascal and I reconnected. One day, we were having a conversation when he mentioned that since his father passed away, his stepmother had deprived him of his inheritance. Apparently, she had found and hidden his father's share certificates, which rightly belonged to him and his brother.

When I heard him say that, I had the same feeling as when the senior manager spoke about the fire. I felt bad for not taking any action when God revealed the situation to me over five years prior. Could I have reduced his waiting time or prevented it altogether by actively intervening on his behalf and informing him about her intentions?

I shared my dream with him and apologized for not discussing it with him over the years. I also joined him in prayer regarding the situation.

Before my encounter with Pascal, I had started to observe a gradual decrease in the frequency of my dreams about other people. I was still having vivid dreams, but most of them were about me. By the time I had this experience with Pascal, the majority of my dreams revolved around myself and my personal circumstances. As a result of not understanding the responsibility attached to the revelations that were given to me about people and their circumstances, they were eventually shut off.

One of the primary reasons I withheld from sharing my dreams was because I did not want to be the "weird guy". In my mind, I thought it was weird to approach a person and, out of the blue, start telling them what you believe you received from God. In a bid to be seen as "cool", I was inadvertently denying an integral aspect of my God-given identity.

The incident with Pascal and the emotional weight of the situation caused me to repent and ask God for mercy. I asked Him to please restore and promised that I would act on revelation as received and led by Him. For a season, there was no change. I was still recalling my dreams, but they were always primarily about my own life situations.

Then one night, I had a dream.

Toilet Encounter Dream

In the dream, I entered a restroom to use it when I saw someone standing somewhat in the dark, masturbating. I looked closely to see who it was, and I realized that it was Thomas. I proceeded to sit on the toilet, and afterwards, he told me how he had been struggling with masturbation for a long time. The dream ended.

When I woke up from this dream, I was elated.

I was elated because God had revealed something to me about another person. It felt like a restoration. This time, I understood the responsibility that came with it. I thought about it for some time and understood that God would have me reach out to Thomas. Thomas was a classmate from school who I had not been in contact with since we left school.

However, I had learned from my past errors and decided that, by whatever means necessary, I would get in touch with him.

I searched on Facebook and saw that we were already connected on the platform. I sent him a message asking for his number, and he responded.

The next day, I called him and spent the time on the phone catching up with him. It was good to reconnect. The following day, I called him again, and it was during this conversation that I decided to bring up the topic highlighted in the dream.

While pondering the dream, I realized that God had embedded the wisdom I needed to successfully navigate this conversation with him in the dream.

A restroom symbolically represents a place of cleansing and repentance. Finding him inside a restroom was indicative of the fact that masturbation was something he was genuinely struggling to overcome but was unable to. *"I proceeded to sit on the toilet, and then he told me."*

Notice the **sequence of events**. I had to sit on the toilet before he told me about his struggles with masturbation. Within the context of the dream, sitting on the toilet was symbolic of me being in a vulnerable state, and it was when I was in a vulnerable state that he in turn shared his struggles with me.

I simply did what I saw myself do in the dream. I started off my conversation with him by speaking about some challenges I had faced in the past and how God had delivered me from them. After sharing, I asked him if masturbation was something he had ever struggled with, and although still shy, he opened up and told me about his struggles with masturbation and his attempts to break free from it. After he confided in me, I shared the dream with him and reassured him that God showed it to me because He wanted Thomas to know that He was aware and wanted to help him break free completely if he would let Him. After praying with him, I offered some counsel based on my own experience, and then I ended the call.

I was overjoyed at the opportunity God had given me to do this, and I genuinely believed that restoration had taken place through the process.

I shared all of this to say: treat as very precious what God reveals to you. Diligently seek His heart concerning why He sent it to you, and be prompt to play your part as He leads you. Make up your mind to always be in a state of readiness to do whatever it may require to fulfil His intended purpose for revealing something to you.

Convey the Redemptive Perspective

I have witnessed numerous instances where an individual has a dream involving another person and decides to inform the person about the dream, but unfortunately, the way the dreamer communicates it unintentionally instills fear and despair in the person's heart.

When sharing a dream, it is crucial to consider the spiritual maturity of the person you are sharing it with. It is important to accurately discern and communicate the redemptive perspective of the dream to prevent any unintended feelings of despair or helplessness.

I must emphasize that this is not a suggestion to modify or manipulate the content of the dream because it is crucial for us to uphold the integrity of the revelation as it was received. However, it is equally important to accurately discern and effectively communicate God's heart on the matter.

CHAPTER 7

God Is Able To Protect You: Dealing with Fear

Dreams are a vivid conduit for revealing spiritual realities, and people who are not anchored in the truth of Jesus Christ's finished work on the cross and the reality of God's inherent power, ability, and willingness to protect them may be frightened by some of the things they see and experience.

Dreams from God are a brutally honest depiction of His perspective on a matter, and He does not sugarcoat matters to protect our sensitivities; instead, He requests for us to come up higher.

This places a demand on us to spend time in His Word so that we may become one with truth. For it is the truth that sets us free (John 8:32).

This raises the question, what is truth?

John 17:17** Sanctify them by your truth; **your word is truth.

The word of God is truth. And because we know that Jesus is the Word, we know that Jesus is truth. (John 14:6)

We must deliberately invest time to study the Word so that we may know who He says we are and what has been made available to us as His children.

A scripture that captures this beautifully is in Ephesians 1:16-20, and I encourage you to spend time asking God to open your eyes to see who you really are in Him and all He has made available to you as His child.

There are several scriptures that, when scrutinized, reveal a simple truth: God is to be trusted, and He is more than able to protect and empower you to overcome all the devices of the enemy.

Adam and Eve in the Garden

God created Adam and Eve and placed them both in the Garden of Eden.

Here are some questions for you to deeply consider: How come satan did not attack them while they were in the garden? Satan already existed before they were created and knew where to find them to tempt them, but never attempted to attack them. Did he suddenly become more powerful after they ate the forbidden fruit?

The answer is no. Satan had no ability to touch them until they "authorized him to" by eating the fruit.

Romans 6:16 *Do you not know that to whom you present yourselves slaves to obey, you are that one's slaves whom you obey, whether of sin leading to death or of obedience leading to* righteousness?

Adam and Eve's actions opened a door. Their disobedience to God was also an agreement with satan and through it, his evil influence became established.

By deception, satan stole Adam's mandate as the god of this world and began to exercise influence and dominion on the earth.

Balaam and Balak

The narrative of Balaam, whom Balak hired to curse the people of Israel, appears in Numbers 22 and 23. God warned Balaam not to go: "You shall not go with them; you shall not curse the people, for they are blessed." However, Balaam's greed pushed him to go with them.

This was the actual statement he made under God's guidance on his first attempt to curse Israel.

Numbers 23:7–8

7. And he took up his oracle and said:

"Balak, the king of Moab, has brought me from Aram.

From the mountains of the east.

'Come, curse Jacob for me,

And come, denounce Israel!'

8. How shall I curse whom God has not cursed?

"And how shall I denounce whom the Lord has not denounced?"

After this attempt, Balaam tried two additional times, and each time, he ended up blessing Israel instead of cursing them. After repeating this cycle and releasing a prophetic word concerning Israel's enemies, he left.

From this scripture, the encounter appears to end here, but in Revelation 2:14, we receive some additional information from Jesus about what Balaam actually did to aid Balak's agenda.

"But I have a few things against you, because you have there those who hold the doctrine of Balaam, who taught Balak to put a

stumbling block before the children of Israel, to eat things sacrificed to idols, and to commit sexual immorality. "

Based on the scripture above, it is evident that Balaam provided advice to Balak regarding a strategy to make the Israelites susceptible to sexual immorality and idolatry. Notice that, despite his best efforts, Balak was not able to cause any harm to the nation of Israel. It was the people themselves who, through their disobedience to God, broke the hedge, and the consequences experienced were a result of their actions.

The efficacy of God's power is so evident in both examples shared above. In both the stories of Adam and Eve in the Garden of Eden and Balaam and the Nation of Israel, their adversary was not able to hurt or attack them until they disobeyed God, thereby proverbially opening the door to the enemy.

Job's Affliction

The story of Job is popular and familiar to most people. In conclusion, Job was a wealthy man who endured terrible adversity, suffered humiliation, and eventually received restoration from God.

There is an important revelation embedded in satan's conversation with God about Job. **Job 1:9-11** *9. So Satan answered the Lord and said, "Does Job fear God for nothing? 10. Have **You** not made a hedge around him, around his household, and around all that he has on every side? You have blessed the work of his hands, and his possessions have increased in the land. 11. But now, stretch out **Your** hand and touch all that he has, and he will surely curse You to Your face!"*

In the scriptures above, satan makes a very significant admission. He was unable to attack Job as a result of God's protective hedge around him. By asking God to stretch His Hand and touch what Job has, satan admits that only God can remove the hedge around Job.

In essence, satan was powerless to afflict Job without God's permission.

Peter's Temptation

Peter's denial of his relationship with Jesus is popular and widely known. Jesus warned Peter ahead of time about this event, and during their conversation, something very significant was revealed.

Luke 22:31(AMP) *Simon, Simon, Listen! Satan has **demanded permission** to sift (all of) you like grain, but I have prayed, (especially) for you (Peter), that your faith (and confidence in me) may not fail.*

Luke 22:31(NKJV) *31. And the Lord said, "Simon, Simon! Indeed, Satan **has asked for you** that he may sift you as wheat. 32.But I have prayed for you that your faith should not fail, and when you have returned to Me, strengthen your brethren."*

It is clear that satan needed to be authorized in order to test both Job and Peter. He could only act within the boundaries of the permission he received. This means that we can always act from a position of peace because we serve a good Father, and if God permits a situation or circumstance in our lives, it will always work out for the best.

It Only Takes One! One of the reasons why the fear of the devil is quite prevalent in a lot of people's hearts is that satan has been unduly elevated in the eyes of people as this incredibly powerful enemy that is at war with God, and all the hosts of heaven are struggling to contain him.

This is a big lie.

One of my favorite scriptures is **Revelation 20:1-3.** *Then I saw **an angel** coming down from heaven, having the key to the bottomless pit and a great chain in his hand. He laid hold of the dragon, that serpent of old, who is the devil and satan, and bound him for a thousand years; and he cast him into the bottomless pit, and shut him up, and set a seal on him, so that he should deceive the nations no more till the thousand years were finished.*

All it takes is ONE Angel!This should help put into proper perspective just how much of an advantage you have as a child of God and should encourage you to boldly follow Him, knowing that your obedience to His word and instructions keeps you fully within His protective hedge.

CHAPTER 8

Interpretation Belongs To God

It is important that, as we seek to consistently interpret our dreams, we do so with a firm understanding that it is God who gives the accurate interpretation of a dream.

There are so many false and misleading dream interpretative models and techniques out there, but if you want to know the accurate meaning of a dream, know that it is The Spirit of God Who empowers us to understand.

This was clearly stated by Joseph on two separate occasions in when he gave interpretations to dreams.

Genesis 40:8 *8. And they said to him, "We each have had a dream, and there is no interpreter of it. So Joseph said to them, "**Do not interpretations belong to God**? Tell them to me, please.*

Genesis 41:15-16

15. Pharaoh said to Joseph, "I have dreamed a dream, and there is no one who can interpret it; and I have heard it said about you that you can understand a dream and interpret it."

*16. Joseph answered Pharaoh, "**It is not in me [to interpret the dream]; God [not I] will give Pharaoh a favorable answer [through me].***

This realization should primarily be established in your heart, thus effectively serving to guide how dreams and their interpretations are approached. Understanding that it is God Who gives the interpretation should serve to remove every burden of performance and help us to posture our hearts correctly to receive from Him.

Hard Truths: Sharing with Integrity

In today's world, there is a prevailing tendency to prioritize political correctness over honesty. The truth is often evaluated and assessed based on how it makes the recipient feel, rather than the actual authenticity of the information being conveyed.

Dreams from God often contain hard truths.

Key Point: Dreams from God are a brutally honest representation of His perspective on a matter.

Within the context of interpreting dreams, it is essential that what God intended by giving a dream is communicated to the dreamer undiluted. Whenever the interpretation of a dream is diluted, the dreamer is denied the opportunity to make the adjustment God intended.

Let us examine how Joseph and Daniel handled difficult dreams given for their interpretation.

The Baker's Dream (Genesis 40:16–19)

When the chief baker saw that the interpretation was good, he said to Joseph, "I was also in my dream, and there were three white baskets on my head. In the uppermost basket were all kinds of baked goods for Pharaoh, and the birds ate them out of the basket on my head." So Joseph answered and said, "This is the interpretation of it: The three baskets are three days. Within three days, Pharaoh will lift off your head from you and hang you on a tree, and the birds will eat your flesh from you. "

From the passage above, we see that the baker's dream foretold his death in three days. This was a very negative outcome, but Joseph simply gave the interpretation of the dream as God had intended. By doing so, Joseph afforded the baker the opportunity to put his house in order and to handle any other business he needed to before his execution. He did not sugarcoat the meaning of the dream, nor did he give him any false hope of a different end.

If Joseph had attempted to embellish or downplay the meaning of the dream, it may have resulted in giving the baker false hope, thereby denying the baker the opportunity to properly prepare for his impending judgment.

Nebuchadnezzar's second dream in Daniel 4:10-26, was a highly sensitive dream. Daniel was tasked with interpreting because the meaning of the dream spelled bad news for a wicked and proud king. This was the same king who executed his magicians for not being able to tell him his first dream. Daniel displayed wisdom by highlighting his loyalty and faithfulness to the king with his initial statement, but then went ahead to accurately interpret the dream as God intended. This required tremendous boldness and a great strength of character from Daniel.

By accurately interpreting the dream and giving the king counsel on how to avoid the judgment that had been decreed, Daniel gave the king an opportunity to repent. Not taking the opportunity was the king's decision, but it was given to him.

I find it interesting that the two people in the Bible who displayed the ability to interpret dreams were also faced with circumstances where excuses could have been made for watering down the truth, but they chose not to.

The following dream provides an excellent illustration of the same idea.

Pepper Soup and Milk

In this dream, we were preparing to host guests, so we were waiting for the ingredients to be delivered. A big bag of pepper was soon delivered from the market. I checked the fresh peppers (other ingredients hadn't been delivered) and asked a little girl in the house to wash them and put them in the freezer to preserve them or blend them before storing. Then I made half a pot of pepper soup with pomo, beef, and some meat that had bones. They were all cut into large chunks.

When the pepper soup was almost ready, I poured some milk into it. Just a few drops would give it a different, creamy taste from the usual pepper soup taste. The little girl had never seen that and didn't know that some soups (she didn't look like she knew about those other soups) are made with milk. So she wondered why I did that. I looked at her and smiled, knowing that she would be gravely disturbed, but I also knew that she would enjoy the taste of the pepper soup when I was done.

I wished she didn't see me doing that so she would not have to go through the agony of thinking about why I'd put milk in pepper soup before tasting it. I had wanted her to taste it and then ask why it was slightly creamy.

Dream Analysis

1 Corinthians 3:2 I have fed you with milk, and not with meat; for hitherto ye were not able to bear it, nor yet now are ye able.

Hebrews 5:12-14 12. For when for the time ye ought to be teachers, ye have need that one teach you again, which be the first principles of the oracles of God, and are become such as have need of milk and not of strong meat. 13. For every one that useth milk is unskillful in the word of righteousness, for he is a babe. 14. But strong meat belongs to them that are of full age, even those who, by reason of use, have their senses exercised to discern both good and evil.

This dream suggests that the dreamer may have reservations about directly conveying certain truths about God and His word to others. As such, there is some dilution to make it "easy" for the hearer to receive. The problem is that while it may make the message easier to hear and maybe even receive, the recipient would not get the full picture of what God intended.

Pepper soup is spicy, and anyone who is going to eat it expects it to be spicy in the mouth. The moment pepper soup is diluted, it loses some of its inherent quality and starts becoming something else. The more diluted it is, the farther away it is from the initial intent and purpose for which it was made.

This is the same as the Word of God. It is important that we deliver the Word of God without diluting its content. There are some hard truths in the Bible, and it's up to us to make sure that the hearer is actually receiving them as God intended.

As we continue to mature on our journey to understanding and interpreting dreams, God will bring people our way who will need assistance. It is important to determine in your heart to say the truth as you understand it and trust God to work out in the person's life whatever needs to be worked out.

CHAPTER 9

Keys to Understanding Your Dreams

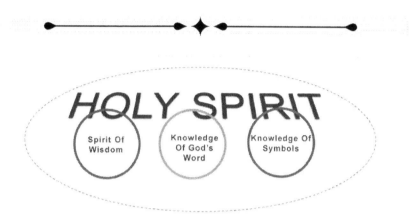

The Holy Spirit Joseph and Daniel are two people in the Bible who displayed a consistent ability to accurately interpret dreams, and both of them were noted for being carriers of The Holy Spirit in their day.

The Spirit of God on Joseph

Genesis 41:37-38

*37. This proposal pleased Pharaoh and all his officials. 38. So Pharaoh asked them, "Can we find anyone like this man, **in whom the Spirit of God abides?"***

The Spirit of God on Daniel:

Daniel 5:11-12

11. There is a man in your kingdom in whom is the Spirit of the Holy God. And in the days of your father, light and understanding and wisdom, like the wisdom of the gods, were found in him; and King

Nebuchadnezzar your father—your father the king—made him chief of the magicians, astrologers, Chaldeans, and soothsayers. 12. In as much as an excellent spirit, knowledge, understanding, interpreting dreams, solving riddles, and explaining enigmas were found in this Daniel, whom the king named Belteshazzar, now let Daniel be called, and he will give the interpretation.

Both Joseph and Daniel were demonstrably filled with The Holy Spirit, and this was acknowledged even by unbelievers!

Attempting to interpret a dream without the help of The Holy Spirit will at best lead to a partial or subjective interpretation, which may leave the dreamer feeling unsatisfied and in need of further clarification. The Holy Spirit is the one who accurately conveys the heart of God and His intent for giving the dream.

The Holy Spirit also assists us in understanding the various elements and symbols present in a dream. This understanding allows us to interpret the dream in a way that effectively communicates God's intended message to the dreamer.

The Spirit of Wisdom

Proverbs 4:7 *Wisdom is the principal thing; therefore, get wisdom and in all thy getting, get understanding.*

The spirit of wisdom is the most crucial component in the pursuit of understanding the mysteries of the kingdom of God, and there is always a price to pay in this pursuit.

In Isaiah 11:2, we see that the spirit of wisdom and understanding are mentioned in the same breath, communicating the essential nature of both working in tandem. The book of Proverbs is especially rich in admonishing the believer to earnestly seek wisdom.

The question to ask is, are you willing to pay the price?

In Kenneth E. Hagin's book, The Believers Authority, he shares his experience of pressing in the place of prayer for the spirit of wisdom based on Paul's prayer in Ephesians 1:17-18.

That the God of our Lord Jesus Christ, the Father of glory, may give to you the spirit of wisdom and revelation in the knowledge of Him, the eyes of your understanding being enlightened; that you may know what is the hope of His calling, what are the riches of the glory of His inheritance in the saints.

Paul didn't pray those prayers only for the church at Ephesus and Colossae. These prayers also apply to us today just as much as they did to the believers at Ephesus because they were given by the Holy Spirit.

In the words of Kenneth Hagin, the turning point in his life came when he prayed these prayers for himself more than **a thousand times**. He personalized the prayers by saying "me" wherever Paul said "you". He spent about six months praying this way during the winter of 1947–1948. Then the first thing he was praying for started to happen. He had been praying for the "spirit of wisdom and revelation" (Ephesians 1:17), and the spirit of revelation began to function! He began to see things in the Bible that he had never seen before. It just began to open up to him.

He advanced more in spiritual growth and knowledge of the Word in those **six months than he had in 14 years** as a minister and in more than 16 years as a Christian.

He said that **this was one of the greatest spiritual discoveries he ever made.**

Notice that the outworking of the spirit of wisdom was evident in his ability to see and understand things that were previously concealed from him in the Word of God. He was determined in his heart to pay the price, and God rewarded his diligent pursuit with understanding.

The Prayers of Paul

After one of our prayer meetings at church, I had a conversation with a friend who works at the church office. He spoke to me about the **Pauline Prayers** and printed them out for me The Pauline Prayers are prayers in the Bible written by Paul to the churches in *Ephesus, Philippi, Colossae,* and from the books of *Thessalonians and Hebrews*. I understood what he said at the time we spoke but it did not really stick with me, so I went home, tucked the prayer booklet in one corner of my room and carried on.

The status quo remained; there was no improvement in my ability to understand, and I was still struggling. Then, about a month later, I had a dream. I perceived that the dream was an instruction to go and speak to my pastor about the matter. While I was waiting in the reception to see the pastor at his office, the same friend who previously spoke to me about and gave me the Pauline prayers started talking to me about dreams and how God had saved him through them. *Coincidence? I think not!*

My interest was piqued! I asked how he was able to understand his dreams, to which he replied, "The Pauline Prayers." He went into detail about how he came to know them; started praying with them diligently, and gradually, his level of understanding and discernment grew.

I immediately knew that it was for this reason that God had asked me to go there. I needed no further impetus to start praying the prayers. God had specifically led me there to help me in the right direction.

It is extremely important to note that these prayers were already in my possession, but because I could not see or understand their value, I left them dormant and completely unused. A lot of times, God has already answered our prayers, but we are unable to see or recognize the answer, so the prayer continues.

A week later, while waiting for my dad's computer to boot up so I could print something, I saw a book on his shelf, The Believers Authority by Kenneth Hagin. I decided to flip through it. The very first chapter of the book is titled **"The Prayers of Paul."** (*Another Coincidence? I think not*).

This great desire caused me to pray, search, study, read, watch, and learn about dreams and the dream interpretative process. I immersed myself in the world of biblical dream interpretation and I soon came across John Paul Jackson's teachings, videos, and books which played a significant role in my journey to biblically understanding and interpreting dreams.

Knowledge of God's Word

At the root of interpreting a dream from God is a very simple premise – the interpreter seeks to make clear what God said. You cannot accurately communicate the heart and intent of someone you do not know, and the primary avenue for learning about God's acts and ways is through His word.

The symbols used to depict different things in our dreams are primarily based on The Word of God. God may use other things to speak to us but the primary reference point is His word and as such, it is very important that we ensure our interpretations line up with the Word of God. This does not mean that we cannot interpret dreams if we do not know the Bible from beginning to the end; this simply means that we need to have enough of His word on our inside, so that it is much easier for the Holy Spirit to bring them to our recollection.

Knowledge of Symbols

Seek to understand the root of things. Learn to understand the innate characteristics of things.

A symbol is something that represents something else—a material object representing something abstract. For example, a snake can be used as a symbol representing a deceptive person. A symbol can be said to be an accurate representation when the innate nature of the symbol chosen accurately matches the subject it has been chosen to represent.

Symbols in dreams can have various interpretations, but our primary source of understanding must be the Word of God. A very good avenue for exposing yourself to a biblical understanding of dream symbols is through the Word of God. The Bible is filled with symbolism, metaphors, similes, and other figurative expressions.

In addition to the word, symbols can also derive their meanings from cultural and colloquial sources.

Get a Biblical dreams dictionary and spend time familiarizing yourself with the Biblical meaning of different symbols. As you continuously expose yourself to the biblical interpretation of symbols, your mind's capacity begins to expand to accommodate better reasoning.

CHAPTER 10

The Art and Process of Dream Interpretation

Learning to interpret dreams is like learning a whole new language. It will take time, and you must be patient with yourself during the process so that you can learn and grow without the added pressure of feeling insufficient or doubting if God is truly with you. No one becomes a master overnight, but as you continue to exercise your senses to accurately discern what God is saying, you will eventually develop maturity in biblical dream interpretation.

My Process: Journey to Interpreting Dreams

When I initially started recollecting my dreams, I had no understanding of them, but I knew that they meant something. I soon started writing them down and sharing them with my mentor. This arrangement worked for a season, as I got the benefit of having my dreams interpreted and being exposed to the dream interpretative process as well. As the frequency of my dreams grew, it became apparent that if I were to rely on another person, I would have a lot of dreams that I would not understand. I needed to know what my dreams meant, and I set out to understand them by deliberately praying, studying, and watching videos of teachings on biblical dream interpretation. This did not lead to an immediate understanding of my dreams; however, God was equipping me with the knowledge of symbolism and the wisdom needed for the dream interpretative process.

It started with an understanding of some parts but not others, a recognition of some symbols and their meaning but not the whole dream. It was a gradual process. Then one day, sitting in the kitchen with my cousin, out of the blue she declared that she had a dream she had been thinking about, and she shared it with me (She had no prior knowledge of my interest in dreams or that I was a dreamer). I had a clear understanding of the dream and told her the meaning as I understood it. It was an awesome feeling.

The very next day, I went to a fellowship I attended at the time, and after the meeting was done, we sat back, talking with each other. During the conversation, one person randomly mentioned that they had a dream some years ago that they had been wondering about (again, this person had no prior knowledge of my interest in dreams). I asked for the dream to be shared, and while I did not understand it all, I understood the main message of the dream.

I had heard these two dreams, and the interpretations came to me quite effortlessly. Something became apparent to me – There was something easier about connecting with the dreams of others than with mine.

The two situations had not been set up by me; I just coincidentally happened to be there when both people were prompted to talk about their dreams. In essence, the Holy Spirit set both situations up and empowered me to interpret.

Biblical Model of Interpretation: The Parable of the Sower Explained

Matthew 13:24-30

*24. Another parable He put forth to them, saying: "The kingdom of heaven is like **a man who sowed good seed** in his **field**; 25. But while men slept, his **enemy** came and **sowed tares** among the wheat and went his way. 26. But when the grain had sprouted and produced a crop, then the tares also appeared. 27. So the servants of the owner came and said to him, 'Sir, did you not sow good seed in your field? How then does it have tares?' 28. He said to them, 'An enemy has done this.' The servants said to him, 'Do you want us then to go and gather them up?' 29. But he said, 'No, lest while you gather up the tares you also uproot the wheat with them. 30. Let both grow together until the harvest, and at the time of harvest I will say to the reapers, "First gather together the tares and bind them in bundles to burn them, but gather the wheat into my barn."*

The Interpretation of this parable is found in Matthew 13:37-43

The **sower of the good seed** is Jesus. **The field** represents the world. **The good seeds** symbolize Christians. **The tares** representing the sinners. **The sower of tares** is the devil.

The **harvest** signifies the end of age. **The reapers** symbolize angels.

In Matthew 13, we see that Jesus gave His disciples (us) the keys for understanding parabolic symbols and applying them for proper interpretation. He first of all starts by giving the context of what He is saying – **The Kingdom of Heaven**.

Without the proper context, it is almost impossible to understand the parable.

This parable can easily be shown to a farmer in a dream, which he will most likely take as a literal warning to avoid a poor harvest. This is his source of livelihood and he can take active steps to avoid what he has been shown. To another person who is a businessman and has made some investments, having a dream of the same parable will end up taking on a more symbolic meaning for him. Once the proper context of the events and elements in a dream are understood, it is much easier to recognize the different elements within it.

That is the starting point.

A lot of mistakes are made in ascribing the wrong meaning to a dream because the context of the dream is not understood. There is usually a clue within the dream to help the dreamer understand what the dream is talking about. Sometimes it is hidden and sometimes it is right there in plain sight.

Sample Dream

*In the dream, I was at a **train station** and it seemed like I was in charge of ensuring that people at the station got on the train when it arrived. I got a signal that the **train** was arriving and I **alerted the people** to come on the train. We got to the platform where people disembark and then those I have called to get on the train come aboard.*

The Symbols in this Dream

The Train station symbolized waiting – a season of waiting and preparation, a time of equipping for what is ahead. *Just as you may get to a train station before the time of your scheduled departure and be required to wait until your departure time arrives, likewise, you* *may find yourself in a season of waiting, where you are being made ready for what God has ahead of you.*

The Train symbolized a vehicle for moving towards God's calling. **Again, the Train** also means to teach and make proficient by instruction or practice.

In this dream, the train has dual meanings – one is evident while the other is hidden in plain sight.

Interpretation The dreamer is in a period of waiting. During that period, he is to prepare and equip others to effectively step into their calling. There is discernment to know and help point out what may not be obvious to others.

A dream is a form of **personal** communication between God and the dreamer. Some symbols used in a dream may oftentimes have a **personal meaning** to the dreamer based on their experiences in that area. It is only God who knows the life history and inclinations of the dreamer and what He has been saying to the dreamer through other means.

A New Way of Thinking

Isaiah 55:9 NKJV *"For as the heavens are higher than the earth, so are My ways higher than your ways and My thoughts higher than your thoughts."*

Dreams from God are not a senseless mash of images put together that we have to try to figure out. There is logic to what God says and does. I love the way John Paul Jackson puts it, "God's logic is a divine logic."

There is indeed logic to dreams from God, and when you understand the accurate interpretation, it ends up making perfect sense to the dreamer, but this process takes time. It will take time to change the natural way you see and perceive things and begin to see and think from God's perspective. Just as the Bible makes clear that as we behold Jesus with eyes of faith, we are transformed and eventually become like Him (2 Corinthians 3:18), I also say that the more you expose yourself to accurately interpreted dreams, the more you begin to understand the dream interpretative process.

Allow yourself ample time to learn and grow. With patience and dedication, you will gradually witness significant improvements in your ability to comprehend and begin to accurately interpret dreams.

Comprehension: A Need to Ponder and Reflect

Comprehension is a very integral part of the dream interpretative process. You cannot accurately interpret a dream if you have not first plainly understood what really occurred in the dream, especially in terms of the true sequence of events and the literal actions that were taken within the dream. Dreams can be highly symbolic, and the words and actions that occur within them play a significant role in the way a dream is interpreted. Thus, if you do not understand what really occurred in the dream, your interpretation will be inaccurate, misleading, and incomplete.

A very effective way to ensure accurate comprehension is to spend time **pondering and reflecting** on the events in the dream in order to make sure that your understanding of the dream accurately reflects what really happened in it.

In order to properly understand these things, time has to be spent analyzing the content and context of the dream. Think through it properly and don't rush to any conclusion. Ask the Holy Spirit to help you see what He is trying to say.

When I initially started interpreting dreams, it took me on average about a week to properly understand and discern what a dream was saying. Sometimes, I would look at it and get a clear picture of the general message but most times when I first took a look at the dream, I would have almost no idea what it was about. In order to understand, I needed to think about it properly. Let it ruminate in my mind and trust the Holy Spirit to unpack it.

I have had experiences of understanding as I listen to the dream but I did not start this way. I have also had experiences of spending hours looking at a dream, praying in tongues, and doing research to understand the meaning of words, animals, places, and contexts, before finally, the light breaks forth and my understanding is fruitful.

The Heart of a Seeker: An Inquisitive Heart That Asks Questions

A very important trait for someone who will interpret dreams is an inquisitive heart—a heart that deliberately probes and questions things with a view to gaining a deeper and more in-depth understanding of things from how they were initially presented. In essence, you do not approach things from a surface-level perspective. You are always aware of the possibility of deeper layers and are willing to pay the price by asking probing questions, seeking information, and researching.

This is the same process at work when trying to interpret a dream. Every aspect of the dream has to be properly scrutinized to ensure that the interpreter has a firm grasp of the events, motives, and actions that occurred within the dream.

Dreams are often like puzzles presented with a surface-level depiction, which requires deliberate probing to unravel the deeper layers hidden underneath the surface.

Pray In Tongues

The ability to pray in tongues is a gift of the Holy Spirit that is very powerful and also greatly misunderstood. In Mark 16:7, Jesus revealed that tongues are a sign that will accompany those who believe in His name. In 1 Corinthians 14:2, we see that when we speak in tongues, no one is able to understand what we are saying except God. In fact, when we pray in tongues, we are speaking mysteries inspired by the Holy Spirit directly to God. This means that as a believer in Jesus Christ, you have access this gift and if you are not able to speak in tongues as a believer, it is something you must earnestly desire and pray for.

After giving my life to Christ, I soon started attending a Pentecostal church, where I became aware of tongues as a gift open to all believers. I earnestly desired to pray in tongues, just like most of the congregation in church, but it seemed like no matter how many times I responded to altar calls to receive the baptism of The Holy Spirit with the evidence of speaking in tongues, nothing seemed to happen. I would stand there, hands would be laid on me, and I would wait for something to happen. I was waiting for the words to jump out of my mouth automatically.

My misunderstanding of the process meant that I went out for numerous altar calls over a period of time, yet nothing changed. The wait continued until one day, when I mentioned it to Pastor Alex over the phone. I shared with him my frustration of going out to be prayed for on numerous occasions and yet never being able to speak in tongues. He then prayed with me over the phone and said to me that God said to tell me that I had already received the baptism of The Holy Spirit and I just needed to speak by faith.

I was ecstatic. You mean, I already had what I had been praying for? He said to simply open my mouth and speak, not from my mind (brain), but to just speak. That was the first time it had been explained to me in a way that I understood. I had always felt like The Holy Spirit was going to speak through me by initiating it. I did not understand that I needed to initiate it and that The Holy Spirit would take over. I started speaking in tongues that day, first by repeating one sound over and over again. As I continued to pray in tongues, my vocabulary expanded and has continued to grow to this day.

Praying in tongues is a gateway to the supernatural realm, and it empowers us to know things. The dream shared below helps to illustrate this truth. The dream is by a good friend who really desired the ability to interpret her dreams but was finding it difficult to grasp. She had purchased and read several books on biblical dream interpretation and had also been praying about it. Despite her best efforts, the struggle to become more proficient persisted, and she earnestly prayed to God to help her begin to interpret. Then she had this dream, which she shared with me.

Transformation through Lifting Dumbbells

*In this dream, I was in my sportswear. I went to my living room, where my brother-in-law was standing by the dining table. On the dining table was a tray with **dumbbells** on it. I said to my brother-in-law, "These are the dumb bells that my friend used to get to where she is in terms of physique." (In real life, the friend had just transformed herself dramatically through workouts from being* *overweight to toned.) I picked up the dumbbells, but they were heavier than I thought. When I used them, I looked in the* **mirror** *and saw my muscles expand significantly. When I went to drop the dumbbells on the tray, I saw* that it *was really a* **torchlight***.*

Key Dream Symbols:

The dumbbells symbolized praying in tongues.

Jude 1:20

But you, beloved, **building yourselves up** *on your most holy faith, praying in the Holy Spirit.*

1 Corinthians 13:1

Though I speak with the tongues of men and of angels, but have not love, I have become sounding brass or a tinkling cymbal(bell).

The mirror symbolized the Word of God.

James 1:23-24

For if anyone is a hearer of the word and not a doer, he is like a man observing his natural face in a mirror.

The torchlight symbolized revelation. A torchlight provides illumination (revelation) when shone in an area that is dark (ignorance).

The Interpretation

The hunger and desire of the dreamer were accurately captured by the outfit she was wearing in the dream. Being in her sportswear was a symbolic indicator of the dreamer's heart posture for what she was requesting from God. The dining table was a place of fellowship and communion. This highlights that praying in tongues is an effective conduit for communion and fellowship with God. The dumbbells were heavy initially to signify the struggles a lot of people face when they first begin to pray in tongues for extended periods. The longer you pray in tongues, the easier it becomes. Seeing her muscles expand significantly in the mirror indicated that the initial proof of growth the dreamer will experience will be evident when reading God's word. A torchlight is used to illuminate any area where there is darkness (ignorance), and this dream highlighted that the dumbbells (tongues) were actually a torchlight (revelation) to see properly.

Discerning an Accurate Interpretation

So you have a dream and have received an interpretation of your dream from someone else. How can you tell that the interpretation you have just received is accurate?

This is a dilemma Pharaoh must have faced when Joseph was summoned to interpret his dream. Pharaoh has no real reason to trust Joseph, as he was a foreigner—a Hebrew who was both a slave and a prisoner—with every potential motivation to lie in order to gain favor and possibly freedom.

To give additional context to this extraordinary encounter between Pharaoh and Joseph, we begin in **Genesis 46:33-34.**

*33. "So it shall be, when Pharaoh calls you and says, 'What is your occupation?' 34. That you shall say, 'Your servants' occupation has been with livestock from our youth even till now, both we and also our fathers,' that you may dwell in the land of Goshen; **for every shepherd is an abomination to the Egyptians.**"*

From the scripture above, it is apparent that Egyptians looked down on Israelites because of their occupation. Not only was Joseph a slave and a prisoner, he was also from a people that were looked down upon by Egyptians, yet Pharaoh believed Joseph's interpretation and elevated him as a result of the wisdom displayed.

Why? Pharaoh believed Joseph's interpretation because, when he heard it, there was a witness in his spirit affirming the accuracy of the interpretation.

When God gives us dreams, He also encodes the accurate interpretation in our spirit; such that when we hear it, there will be an inner peace and witness that what we have heard is true.

The inverse is also true; when an interpretation is inaccurate or fails to address the crux of the matter encoded in a dream, there will be a niggling unease in the heart of the dreamer suggesting that what they heard is incomplete or completely wrong and misleading. The key is to pay attention to your spirit to accurately discern the authenticity and accuracy of what you have received.

The Lord's Divine Logic at Work: The Interpretation Will Make Sense Once Revealed

The mystery of a dream remains while it is yet to be understood, but the moment it has been interpreted, the dream and its interpretation should actually make logical sense to the dreamer as they think and ponder on it.

Let us take a look at Pharaoh's two dreams and Joseph's interpretations of them.

Dream 1

Genesis 41:17-21

17. Then Pharaoh said to Joseph: "Behold, in my dream I stood on the bank of the river.

18. Suddenly seven cows came up out of the river, fine looking and fat; and they fed in the meadow.

19. Then behold, seven other cows came up after them, poor and very ugly and gaunt, such ugliness as I have never seen in all the land of Egypt.

20. And the gaunt and ugly cows ate up the first seven, the fat cows.

21. When they had eaten them up, no one would have known that they had eaten them, for they were just as ugly as at the beginning. So I awoke.

Dream 2

Genesis 41:22-24

22. Also I saw in my dream, and suddenly seven heads came up on one stalk, full and good.

23. Then behold seven heads, withered, thin, and blighted by the east wind, sprang up after them.

24.And the thin heads devoured the seven good heads. So I told this to the magicians, but there was no one who could explain it to me."

Joseph's Interpretation

Genesis 41:25-31

25. Then Joseph said to Pharaoh, "The dreams of Pharaoh are one; God has shown Pharaoh what He is about to do:

26. The seven good cows are seven years, and the seven good heads are seven years; the dreams are one.

27. And the seven thin and ugly cows which came up after them are seven years, and the seven empty heads blighted by the east wind are seven years of famine.

28. This is the thing which I have spoken to Pharaoh. God has shown Pharaoh what He is about to do.

29. Indeed seven years of great plenty will come throughout all the land of Egypt;

30. But after them seven years of famine will arise, and all the plenty will be forgotten in the land of Egypt; and the famine will deplete the land.

31. So the plenty will not be known in the land because of the famine following, for it will be very severe.

The **dreams' interpretation keys** were **seven good cows and seven good heads,** which symbolized seven years of abundance and prosperity, as well as **seven ugly cows and seven empty heads,** which symbolized seven years of lack and famine.

One of the most remarkable aspects of Pharaoh's dream is the dilemma presented in each scenario, where the ugly cows swallowed the beautiful cows and maintained their ugliness. The contrasting picture in this scene not only captures our attention but also provides insight into the severity of what was about to happen.

Joseph's interpretation sheds light on a symbolic picture that, in human terms, appears nonsensical. How can an ugly and famished entity swallow something large and beautiful yet still remain ugly and famished afterwards?

Joseph's interpretation revealed that the seven years of famine would be incredibly destructive to the point where the abundance of the preceding seven years would be completely overshadowed and forgotten. This metaphorically implies that the devastation caused by the famine would erase any memory of the previous years of plenty.

Interpretation is crucial to understanding a seemingly illogical puzzle that initially appears nonsensical. However, once accurately interpreted, the puzzle becomes perfectly understandable.

CHAPTER 11

The Importance Of Context In Dream Interpretation

Context is Key

The ability to understand the context in which things occur in a dream is absolutely critical to accurately interpreting the dream. Any attempt to interpret a dream without first understanding the context will likely lead to an erroneous interpretation.

For example, consider the scenario below:

Linda suddenly felt a hard shove from Rachel and next thing she knew, she was on the lawn. "What did you do that for?" Linda screamed.

1. The questions that you should answer are: What do you think of Rachel after reading the events depicted above?

2. Why do you think she shoved Linda?

3. What do you think of Linda after reading the events depicted above?

The Full Context

Linda and Rachel set out for a walk. As they were walking, Rachel noticed a manhole in Linda's path. Seeing that Linda had her earphones on and was engrossed in a game on her mobile phone, Rachel made the split-second decision to push Linda out of the pathway of the manhole. Linda suddenly felt a hard shove from Rachel, and the next thing she knew, she was on the lawn.

"What did you do that for?" Linda screamed.

By looking at and considering the full context, it is easier to see that Rachel was not ill-intentioned towards Linda. She was actually trying to save her by moving her out of harm's way.

At first, there wasn't enough information to properly consider and understand Rachel's motivation; hence, some guesses and insinuations are required to attempt to understand.

Likewise, when trying to interpret a dream, it is important that we consider all aspects depicted in the dream and seek to interpret the symbols and actions within the context in which they occurred. An inability or unwillingness to consider context almost always leads to an erroneous interpretation.

I have seen situations where people make blanket statements like, "Seeing yourself in school in a dream represents backwardness." It is erroneous to apply a one-size-fits-all interpretation based on a symbol without taking into consideration the context of the dream.

Symbols often have multiple meanings, and the examples provided below help illustrate this concept more clearly.

Learning to Determine Context

Dream Scenario 1

*James walks into a board meeting, and all the attendees are already seated. Just then, he glances downward and notices that he has no **shoes** on.*

Dream Scenario 2

*James walks into the living room, which has a beautiful rug laid out on the floor. As he is about to initiate a conversation with his father, his father asks James to take off his **shoes** before speaking.*

Dream Scenario 3

*James is at the entrance of a formal work event, and at the security checkpoint, he is informed that he has the **wrong pair of shoes on** and needs to change to another pair that is presented to him. He takes a look at the shoes and recognizes that they belong to Tom, who is his boss at work. He puts the shoes on, and they initially feel too big for him, but as he walks around in them, he becomes more comfortable walking in them.*

What do you think shoes represent in each exercise?

In scenario 1, a careful reflection of the event shows that James got to the meeting late, as everyone was **already** seated when he arrived.

Ephesians 6:15

Having shod your feet with the preparation of the gospel of peace…

Considering the context, the most suitable interpretation is from the scripture in Ephesians 6:15, which likens **preparation** to a **shoe** that is fastened to one's feet to make the path ahead easier to navigate.

James' lack of shoes was symbolic of a **lack of preparation**.

In scenario 2, a scripture that comes to mind is **Exodus 3:5.** 5. *Then He said, do not draw near this place. Take your sandals off your feet, for the place where you stand is holy ground.*

In a dream, your father can be a symbolic representation of God because God is depicted as a father in the Bible. When we consider the sequence of events, we see that it has a close correlation with the events at the burning bush where Moses encountered God for the first time.

Within that context, God asked Moses to **remove his shoes as a sign of reverence,** just as James' Father asked him to remove his shoes before speaking.

In scenario 3, it is evident that the primary context of the dream is a work-related event. This context serves as the backdrop against which all other elements of the dream can be observed. Wearing Tom's shoes can be compared to *filling his shoes*, an idiomatic expression that means taking someone else's position.

In the context of this dream, shoes symbolize a specific **position** or **role**.

Symbols Derive Meaning Based on Context

The three dream scenarios shared above have similar symbols in them; **a lack of shoes** and **putting on shoes**. These similarities notwithstanding, the interpretation for each of the dreams was very different. This is because the context in which shoes were depicted in each dream example was very different.

Every symbol has multiple potential meanings. Take a look at these symbols below and their different potential meanings.

1. **Serpent**

A serpent could symbolize:

- **Deception**: Our first introduction to the serpent is in Genesis 3, and its first action was to **deceive** Eve (**Gen 3:1-7**).
- **Lies**: The serpent told Eve a massive **lie,** which **deceived** her and caused grave consequences.
- **A long tail or tale**: The bigger the **tail or tale**, the bigger the lie.
- **Curse**: As a result of the serpent's action, God placed a **curse** on the serpent (**Gen 3:14**).
- **Satan**: is also known as "the serpent of old" (**Rev 12: 9**).
- **Slander**: **Psalm 140:3** reads, "They have sharpened their tongues like a serpent; adders **poison** is under their lips."
- **Salvation/Jesus: Numbers 21: 8** reads, "Then the Lord said to Moses, 'Make a fiery serpent, and set it on a pole; and it shall be that everyone who is bitten, when he looks at it, shall live.'" **John 3:14-15** also says, "And as Moses lifted up the serpent in the wilderness, even so must the Son of Man be lifted up. That whoever believes in Him should not perish but have eternal life."

How to Determine the Context

The help of the Holy Spirit is critical to being able to properly discern and understand what a dream is talking about. I have found that a lot of times (not all the time), the Holy Spirit will help you based on what you know. He will help you to connect the hidden dots and bring the symbols to life, thereby piecing it all together. In order for the Holy Spirit to speak to you about the meaning of the symbols, most times, He requires you to have some understanding of what the symbols mean and how their meanings are derived.

I have personally attempted to interpret dreams by relying solely on symbol dictionaries. This involved searching for each symbol, writing out their potential meanings, and analyzing them. However, I can confidently say that this process does not work. Without the help of The Holy Spirit, all you will end up with are a bunch of symbols with no cohesive message.

God speaks a lot of times in parables, especially in dreams, and most dreams are symbolic. This means that the elements contained within the dreams are usually representative of something else other than that which is presented.

A house sometimes represents a person. A car sometimes represents a person's life or progress. A lion sometimes represents Jesus Christ.

At other times, a house represents a house. A car represents a hindrance. A lion represents satan.

How do we then determine which meaning to assign to a symbol? The context.

Learning Point: The context within which the symbol is used is what determines what meaning to assign to the symbol.

This dream helps to illustrate the role of context:

In the dream, I was on a street that was somewhat dark. There was a yellow school bus parked on the street, absolutely sitting still. I was not happy and tried to notify anyone that the school bus was illegally parked. I thought to myself, that if I saw a policeman, I would report him.

As I walked past the school bus that was completely motionless, I saw that it was full of children, with the bus driver sitting in his seat. The bus was full, but there wasn't any sign of life there; everyone just sat completely still, including the bus driver. This bus was on my right. On my left, there were a lot of yellow school buses parked on the sidewalk of the street, and more were getting ready to park. With the way they were parked, it looked almost impossible for any of them to come out, as the ones just coming in were blocking the ones already parked.

Within the context of the dream, the yellow school bus is representative of a teaching ministry.

First off, the school bus is described with a color – yellow. The first question to ask should be, "Is the color relevant to the meaning of the bus?" In America and some other countries of the world, the school buses which transport nursery to high school students to school are painted yellow. So, a yellow school bus naturally brings to mind a certain age range of the occupants. Another way of describing this is their maturity level.

"I noticed that the bus was filled with children, and the bus driver was seated in the front."

This line from the dream corroborates the meaning of the yellow school bus, thus emphasizing that the yellow serves to highlight the maturity level of the occupants on the bus.

The Importance of Accurately Discerning the Context of a Dream

A lot of people have had dreams of encouragement and great victory which should ideally have propelled them to continue on the path they were already on, but an inability to accurately interpret and a predisposition of viewing spiritual things from a lens of fear, has robbed a lot of people of the peace and encouragement, God initially intended.

A pastor once shared with me a message that he had received from a friend. This message was about a dream that the friend had regarding the pastor."Bros, pray seriously concerning the attack of death against your life. I saw you rejoicing at the finishing line after running a good race. It has various interpretations but I had to pray against death because your wife and kids still need, you even though it is sweeter to be at home with the Lord. I have prayed for you. You can also take it up in prayer."

The first question to ask to properly distill this message is, "What did the person actually see?"

In this case, the person saw the pastor **rejoicing** at the **finishing line** after **running a good race**. This was the actual revelation. Everything else that was included in the message was the dreamer's perception of what he saw after he woke up. The dreamer, out of nowhere, conjured up a cause for alarm based on a faulty understanding of the dream's context.

Another very important thing to note is that the reported dream was incomplete. The dreamer removed a portion of his entire dream that he felt was relevant to the pastor and sent it to him. By doing this, the context in which he saw the pastor rejoicing at the finishing line was lost in translation.

Key Point: It is indeed possible that God showed the dreamer the pastor as a wake-up call to get his act together and ensure that he lines up with this pastor. It may also have been an affirmation to the dreamer that his pastor friend is on the right path to finishing in glory. This dream served as an affirmation to the dreamer about his pastor friend and to confirm that his destination is indeed Christ.

Regardless of how you look at this dream, there was absolutely no basis to ask for serious prayers against the attack of death.

Learning Point: It is important to clearly differentiate between what was actually seen and the perception of what was seen.

95

CHAPTER 12

Emotions in Dreams

A lot of people have dreams where they are happy and excited during the dream, but when they wake up, they become afraid because of their perception of what occurred in the dream. During a dream, the emotions displayed are a real reflection of the symbolic significance of what occurred. However, when you wake up from a dream, your mind kicks in and begins to process the information based on cultural nuances and your natural predisposition, which may be contrary to what was depicted in the dream.

Someone once shared this dream with me. *In the dream, I was on the beach, chilling with a crowd—mostly people from church, some friends, and some strangers. The tide was coming in more and more. When it finally did, I dove into the water. Upon getting into the water, it felt like being in a huge water tank with a little opening at the top. I held my breath for so long that people were worried when I surfaced. I dove again, and this time I had a bit of difficulty coming up. My mother sent down a rope for me to pull myself up. I then became comfortable and dove a lot, even dancing under the water to Don Moen's song, Give Thanks.*

I woke up with the song playing in my head, but then fear set in as I realized how scary and dangerous diving was.

John 7:38-39:

*He who believes in Me, as the Scripture has said, out of his heart will flow **rivers of living water**." But this He spoke concerning the **Holy Spirit**.*

We see that **water** can be used symbolically to represent the Holy Spirit.

In the dream, they were **on the beach**. This sets the scene of the dream and provides a context within which everything taking place should be analyzed. The beach water represents The Holy Spirit.

The tide coming in more represents the move of the Spirit, and the dreamer **diving in** symbolizes diving into Him. The dreamer's action in the dream dispels any notion of the water being dangerous. If the water was dangerous or perceived to be dangerous, the dreamer would have taken off running.

The dreamer **dove in again**. By diving back in, it clearly shows that the dreamer must have liked being in there. This dispels any notion of danger, at least to the knowledge of the dreamer. The dreamer goes on to **dance under the water**, particularly to Don Moen's song. This gives further context to the actions of the dreamer. In God, a thankful heart and disposition come naturally; it is much easier. This portion of the dream may have been an answer to a prayer by the dreamer for a more thankful disposition.

Fear set in when the dreamer woke up. Dreams that have extremely striking images or actions may generally induce some form of fear or at least apprehension when we wake up and begin to think about them, but what is actually most important is how we felt during the dream! If the dreamer was not afraid of the water in the dream, kept jumping back into it, and praised God while underneath the water, then surely there was something about that water that at the very least facilitates fellowship with God.

1 Corinthians 2:14

But the natural man does not receive the things of the Spirit of God, for they are foolishness to him, nor can he know them because they are spiritually discerned.

To minimize fear, it is advisable to detach oneself from the instinctive mind and its tendencies. It is beneficial to adopt a scriptural and symbolic approach when interpreting a dream, regardless of the perceived danger within it. A natural interpretation of a situation in a dream may give a clue, but it can be extremely misleading, as a lot of natural interpretations do not have any scriptural context embedded in them.

> **Key Point:** It is always important to note the way you feel in the dream. Within the dream, your emotions are a true representation of the event you are seeing and are often key to understanding the true meaning of the dream. It is also important to pay special attention to what you say as well. Most of the time, the dreamer's utterances reveal the true position and state of the event they are witnessing.

Is it literal or symbolic?

There are various types of dreams. Some dreams are literal, meaning they will occur exactly as shown to the dreamer. Other dreams are symbolic, containing hidden meanings that can only be deciphered by understanding the symbols used in the dream. Additionally, there are dreams that have both a literal and symbolic meaning.

It is essential that we properly discern which it is and apply the interpretation accordingly.

Literal Dreams

One of the most simple rules to follow is that if the actions in a dream are naturally possible and do not include any obvious symbolic elements, then the dream can be interpreted literally. For example, in a dream, a person may find themselves driving to work in their actual car. However, during the journey, an unfortunate accident occurs.

In this dream, all the elements can be interpreted literally. Although there is no guarantee that it will happen exactly as shown, there is a higher probability of it occurring.

Symbolic Dreams

Let us use an example similar to the one above, but with an additional element. In a dream, a person finds themselves driving to work in the same car they use in their everyday life. While driving, he has a collision with a ship on the road.

This dream becomes symbolic right away because it is highly improbable, if not completely impossible, for a ship to be on a road.

Both Literal and Symbolic Dreams

Still using the same example, a person has a dream where they are driving to work in the same car they use in their everyday life. On his way, he picks up a few co-workers and they engage in conversation. During the conversation, an argument arises that leads to him losing concentration and getting into an accident.

The dream can hold both a literal and symbolic significance, and it's essential that we lean on the Holy Spirit to help us discern the full meaning of the dream.

The literal meaning would be for the person to pray, be careful, pay attention, and avoid arguments while driving. The **symbolic meaning** would be a warning to the dreamer about the importance of exercising caution when choosing individuals to accompany them on their journey. In essence, he is to avoid those who may create conflict and distract him from achieving his goal.

One category of dreams where there is a strong need for discernment and restraint is usually one that contain people familiar to us. The majority of the time, the person in your dream is symbolically chosen based on a combination of the way you perceive the person and the message God is trying to pass across to you.

Learning Point: About 90% of your dreams are about you.

Most times, God uses a person's actions and our reaction in a dream to show us how we react in certain situations. The dream is not about the other person; **it is about you.**

Key Point: Dreams are a brutally honest representation of God's perspective on a matter.

CHAPTER 13

Marriage in Dreams

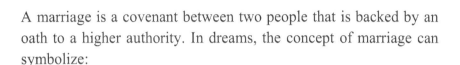

A marriage is a covenant between two people that is backed by an oath to a higher authority. In dreams, the concept of marriage can symbolize:

- a literal union between two individuals,

- a spiritual connection,

- the relationship between Christ and the church

- a bond with Christ,

- a business partnership or merger,

- a soul tie that can be either godly or ungodly.

Ephesians 5:27 ... *a church in all her glory without spot or wrinkle, but that she should be holy and blameless.*

Revelation 19:7 *Let us rejoice and exult and give Him the glory, for the marriage of The Lamb has come and His bride has* **made herself ready.** *It was granted her to clothe herself with fine linen, bright and pure – For the fine linen is the righteous deed of the saints.*

Dreams where you see yourself getting ready for an unknown or unseen groom, or have challenges with your wedding dress, or struggle with the lack of a dress, may not be talking about a physical husband or wedding. More importantly, they may be addressing your current preparedness for Christ's return.

Seeing yourself in a dream wearing a stunning, immaculate white wedding dress may not necessarily symbolize a literal marriage. Instead, it could serve as a reminder of what Jesus Christ, the Bridegroom, expects from you upon His return

A wedding ceremony acts as the gateway into a marriage. Therefore, dreams that focus on problems on the wedding day may indicate obstacles to marriage in the life of the dreamer.

Dreams serve as a pathway for emotions and mindsets that we typically suppress in our everyday lives. Through dreams, these suppressed aspects of ourselves begin to find expression, offering us valuable insights into the inner workings of our hearts, and revealing our true emotional state. If you find yourself complaining about marriage, the opposite sex, commitment, or similar topics in a dream, it could indicate that your true thoughts and feelings about marriage are being reflected in your dream.

When it comes to being engaged in a dream, it could potentially signify a real-life engagement. Moreover, similar to how marriage can symbolize a business partnership, a covenant, or a strong agreement, a dream proposal or engagement may also symbolize events that come before and lead to these situations.

Related Symbols on Marriage:

An engagement ring signifies a bride of Christ, a marriage covenant, strong commitment, or a seal of God's promise.

A bridesmaid or groomsman symbolizes helpers. They assist in ensuring the success of the ceremony by preparing the bride or groom. Similarly, this can also represent pastoral care, prophetic guidance, and other related aspects. The primary emphasis is on offering help.

Being the bride of Christ illustrates how Jesus paid the ultimate price for man, so that we may be restored and given the opportunity to choose to fear, obey, and keep God's commands. There remains a requirement to make ourselves ready in preparation for His return. This requirement is often communicated through dreams in which we see ourselves in wedding dresses.

Dreaming about "The One"

In my dream, I was in a room with Cynthia, Rolake, and Tayo. Rolake started crying, but they were tears of joy. She asked me to give her my full name, which I did. The impression I got in the dream was that God had spoken to her that I was to marry her son, Toju, and she was happy because she had been waiting.

The next day, Toju called me, and we spoke over the phone about ourselves. As we were still on the phone, we realized that we were standing in front of each other. I was sitting on the bonnet of a white car. He entered a different white car and left, and I entered my own white car and left.

I got home, and Kemi was in my room. We both spoke about Obaro because it seemed like she had also dated him. She spoke about how he was caring, but the last time they broke up and she wanted to get back with him, he gave her the condition that they had to indulge in abnormal intimacy practices. That was what deterred her. I explained to her that when Obaro and I were dating, anytime we were intimate, he would try to include abnormal practices, and I would scream at him to get off, and it would lead to a fight. We concluded that it wasn't ideal to date Obaro anymore.

Later, I laid on my mom's bed, and she gave me an invitation card. It was the most beautiful invitation card I had ever seen. It had different pastel colors with cloud patterns and glitters on it. By the time I read it, I discovered that it was a WEDDING INVITATION for Toju and me. The wedding was to hold at Rolake's sister's house, and it said something about a prophetic wedding. This invitation card had a lot of heavenly words that I cannot remember.

I was so surprised, and my mouth was wide open. I expressed my concern about the wedding being too soon to my mother, and she replied that it was not because Rolake heard directly from God and it was time. She continued, saying that with God, there's nothing like a dating period, and Rolake hears from God things that other people don't.

The Interpretation

The key to understanding this dream lies in the meaning of the main character's name.

The full name for Toju is *Toriseju,* which means *God's will is supreme.* The essence of the dream was to communicate to the dreamer the need to "marry" God's will and make it supreme in her life. *Obaro*, on the other hand, means progress. Obaro, an ex in the dream, represents the way the dreamer made progress in the past, which included a need to compromise. With these two keys, it becomes easy to recognize what God was communicating through the dream.

Some people have found themselves trapped by a dream they had, which seemingly appeared to show or confirm who their spouse is, and they end up waiting endlessly for the manifestation of something that may or may not occur.

Marriage is a big deal, and as Christians, it is ideally a once-in-a-lifetime affair, so no one wants to make a mistake. We all want to know God's will, and rightly so. The question is, does having a dream with you and someone known to you at the altar constitute an instruction on who to get married to?

Not necessarily.

Aside from the fact that it may or may not be a God-given dream, it is also important to remember that dreams are usually symbolic. The people we see in our dreams are sometimes a symbolic representation of what God is trying to speak to us about. There are no hard-and-fast rules and it is always best to rely on the Holy Spirit for guidance.

Dreaming of a **husband** may represent **God** or **Christ.**

Dreaming of a **wife** may represent the **church.**

Dreaming of **marriage** may represent a covenant.

There is therefore the possibility that the dream may be from God and is indeed a genuine confirmation, or it may be from God but only a symbolic representation that will effectively convey His intended message to you. Alternately, it might just be a dream that you conjured up on your own as a result of your mind's obsession with the concept.

Key Point: It is best to have confirmation before standing on a dream, especially for major life decisions.

2 Corinthians 13:1 *"This will be the third time I am coming to you. "By the mouth of **two or three witnesses, every** word shall be established."*

God always confirms His Word; He doesn't leave us hanging. This scripture is very important because it acts as a safeguard for people who are genuinely trying to follow His lead.

As with all things, there are no hard and fast rules; we truly must rely on The Holy Spirit at all times, and He will lead us to all truth. The Word of God contains wisdom that will help us avoid a lot of the traps and pitfalls set for us along the way.

For a female, having a dream about getting married to a guy who has not made his intentions clear, is not in an exclusive relationship with you, or is currently dating another person is reason to tread with caution. Be careful what you make of the dream, and instead seek God to speak clearly to you. If it is of Him and by Him, He will confirm His word.

CHAPTER 14

Colors in Dreams

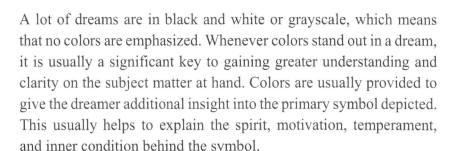

A lot of dreams are in black and white or grayscale, which means that no colors are emphasized. Whenever colors stand out in a dream, it is usually a significant key to gaining greater understanding and clarity on the subject matter at hand. Colors are usually provided to give the dreamer additional insight into the primary symbol depicted. This usually helps to explain the spirit, motivation, temperament, and inner condition behind the symbol.

Dream of the Old House

In the dream, I remember being in a car with Patricia at the gate of our former house in Alabama. Linda wanted to drive, in so I got out of the car to open the gate for her. She was in a maroon-red Honda Accord. When we opened the gate for Linda, she sped into the compound and almost hit the garage gate, so we both looked at her, quite surprised.

Learning Point: The **former house** represents a past experience that occurred at the house depicted in the dream. The house serves as a frame of reference for the time the dream refers to. The dreamer **opening the gate** showed that he was allowing or inviting Linda in to share in that experience for a purpose not expressly stated. A **car** represents ministry.

From the symbols listed above, we can get an idea of what the dream pertains to, but Linda's action remains a mystery. What is the underlying motivation for her action? The key to the complete interpretation of this dream lies in the color of the car. It helps to explain why she *almost* hit the gate.

The color **red** symbolizes passion or zeal.

The Interpretation

The dreamer shared a childhood experience with Linda, which was depicted through the opening of the gate of her former house for Linda to drive in.

Linda drove in rather aggressively and almost hit the gate, which is symbolic of trying to help with the situation but rubbing the dreamer off the wrong way because of how direct her approach was.

In this context, the maroon-red color represents passion and helps us better understand the motivation behind Linda's approach. Linda did not mean to rub the dreamer off the wrong way; she was simply passionate about trying to help and in the process, she came across as brash to the dreamer.

Patricia appeared to be in the dream quite randomly, but she wasn't. She had had a similar childhood experience as the dreamer and her presence in the dream was to help the dreamer accurately discern what the dream was really about.

Learning Point: People in our dreams who are with us in confined areas are often partakers of something similar to what the dream refers to.

Below is a list of some colors and the interpretations attached to them:

1. Red

Red symbolizes **power.**

Revelation 6:4 *And there went out another horse that was red, and power was given to him that sat thereon to take peace from the earth, and that they should kill one another, and there was given unto him a great sword.*

When someone gets angry, a common way to describe that person is to say that they are seeing red or they are red hot with anger. Thus, another symbol for red is **anger.**

The red light on a traffic light stands for **stop or danger.** This could also translate to dreams. Furthermore, **passion** and **zeal** are inferred meanings of the color, which are derived from anger and romance.

Red could also represent **sin.**

Isaiah 1:18

"Come now, and let us reason together," says the Lord, "Though Your sins are like scarlet (red), they shall be as white as snow; though they are red like crimson, they shall be as wool."

Another interpretation for red is **blood,** and since the life of a thing is in the blood, **life** is also an inferred meaning of red.

2. Yellow:

Yellow symbolizes a **gift.**

Psalm 68:13 *Though you lie down among the sheepfolds, You will be like the wings of a **dove** covered with silver, And her feathers with **yellow** gold.*

Luke 3:22 *And the **Holy Spirit** descended in bodily form like a **dove** upon Him, and a voice came from heaven which said, "You are My beloved Son; in You I am well pleased."*

Acts 2:38 *Then Peter said to them, "Repent, and let every one of you be baptized in the name of Jesus Christ for the remission of sins; and you shall receive **The Gift of the Holy Spirit.***

From the three scriptures above, we can see that, the dove is a symbol of the Holy Spirit, the Holy Spirit is both a gift and a giver of **gifts** (the nine gifts of the Spirit), and the color used to describe His symbolic nature is yellow-gold.

An additional meaning of Yellow is **fear, cowardice, impending danger** or a need to **watch out.**

3. Blue

Blue represents **something heavenly, the spirit or something spiritual**. It could also refer to **depression** or **healing**.

Exodus 28:31 *You shall make the robe of the ephod all of blue.*

This scripture signifies the color of Aaron's robe, which he wore while serving in God's presence at the temple. The temple built on earth was a replica of the **heavenly** temple.

Genesis 1:1 *In the beginning, God created the heavens and the earth.*

The color of the sky that was used to divide the heavens is blue. The blue sky is composed of air which symbolizes spirit; therefore, blue can also be symbolic of **spirit** or **spiritual**.

Someone who is complaining or lamenting about their suffering and depression, or generally going through a rough season can be said to be **singing the blues**.

Proverbs 20:30 *The **blueness** of a wound cleanseth away evil.*

This verse indicates that blue can serve as a symbol of **healing.**

More often than not, the most common interpretation for the color blue in a dream is something spiritual or heavenly.

CHAPTER 15

People in Dreams

People often play significant roles in our dreams, and it may be quite challenging at first to accurately identify what their presence in our dreams really mean.

Sybolisms attached to a person in your dream may be:

1. The meaning of their name.

2. What predominantly comes to mind when you think of them?

3. The actual person.

To understand the concept of people representing the meaning of their name, we have to do a deeper dive into the subject of names and what they really represent.

What is in a Name?

I attended a Catholic church with my parents while growing up, and as part of the process of getting baptized in the church; we had to pick a name. I was already in secondary school at the time and got to choose my name. I chose Michael.

Guess why? Michael Jackson.

I liked the way his name sounded and the person it was associated with, so I chose the name.

This is how a lot of people in different parts of the world give names to their children today. They pick a sound they like and assign it to their child without a full understanding or regard for the full import of their choice. A name is not just a sound used to identify a person or a thing; a name actually conveys and provokes a spiritual reality based on its meaning.

The Israelites recognized the significance of names. In fact, names are so significant that God Himself either named or renamed each of the three Patriarchs of our faith.

Abraham

Gen 17:5 *No longer shall your name be called Abram but your name shall be Abraham;* ***for I have made you a father of many nations.***

Abram: Exalted Father ---------> **Abraham:** Father of a multitude

Isaac

Genesis 17:19 *Then God said: No. Sarah your wife shall bear you a son and you shall call his name Isaac; i will establish my covenant with him for an everlasting covenant and with his descendants after him.*

Named By God ----------> **Isaac:** He Laughs

Jacob

Genesis 32:28 *And He said, your name shall no longer be called* ***Jacob but Israel.*** *For you have struggled with God and with men and have prevailed.*

Jacob: Heel holder /supplant -----------> **Israel**: God prevails.

From the examples above, we see that God was deliberate in naming each of them and they lived up to the meaning of their names. Abram means exalted father, yet, had no children, but God changed his name to Abraham which was a reflection of the promise over his life. Abraham became a Father of a mighty multitude just as his name connoted.

Another example of note is Nabal who acted wickedly against David's men. As a result David rode out with the intention of killing him. Nabal's wife, Abigail rode out to appease David and during the exchange she shared something very profound about her husband, Nabal.

1 Samuel 25:25 Please let not my Lord regard this scoundrel Nabal. For as his name is, so is he: Nabal is his name, and folly is with him! But I, your maidservant did not see the young men of my lord whom you sent.

Nabal means fool and Abigail indicated that her husband, Nabal was acting in accordance with his name.

A name is therefore not just a sound, but conveys a spiritual reality based on its meaning and this principle brings us to the first way of identifying a person in a dream.

1. **A Person Representing the Meaning of Their Name**.

In a dream, a person named Emmanuel may actually be a symbolic depiction of Jesus in that dream; likewise someone named Mercy in a dream may be a symbolic depiction of the dreamer receiving mercy or the absence of mercy depending on the context of the dream.

2. What Comes To Mind When You Think Of Them?

Rachel had a dream in which she saw herself getting married to her ex-boyfriend. What could this dream possibly indicate, given that their relationship ended on a sour note?

After hearing her recount the dream in its entirety, I asked her what immediately came to mind when she thought of her ex, and her response was, "He's a pathological liar."

The next step was to ascertain if she had been struggling with consistently telling the truth recently, and her response was affirmative. She had found herself lying more than she usually would.

God used her marriage to a pathological liar in the dream as a metaphor depicting the true effects of choosing to lie repeatedly. By making the choice to lie in different circumstances, she was choosing to enter into an agreement with lying.

3. A person in a dream is not always symbolic.

In a dream, a person may simply portray themselves.

Some Commonly Misunderstood Aspects of Dreams

Matthew 6:26 *Look at the birds of the air, for they neither sow nor reap nor gather into barns; yet **your** heavenly **Father** feeds them. Are you not of more value than they?*

Isaiah 54:5:

*For your **Maker** is your **husband,** The Lord of hosts is His name; and your Redeemer is the Holy One of Israel; He is called the God of the whole earth.*

118

Ephesians 5:25: *Husbands, love your **Wives**, as **Christ** loved the **church** and gave himself up for her.*

John 10:14 *I am the good **shepherd;** and I know My **sheep**, and am known by My own.*

Your **father** may represent **God** or an authority figure in your life.

Your **husband** may also represent **God** or **Jesus**

Your **wife** may represent the **church**.

Your **pastor** may represent **God or Christ**

Your **pastor's wife** may represent the **church**.

Other common symbolic representations of people include:

- **Baby**: New, beginning, new idea, or new work or project.
- **Doctor**: Healer, Christ, or pastor.
- **Giant**: Strongman, stronghold, challenge, obstacle, or need for spiritual warfare.
- **Grandmother** or **Grandfather**: Spiritual inheritance, which may be good or evil.
- **Mother:** The source of a thing or the church.
- **Soldier**: Spiritual warfare, angel, or demon.
- **Brother**: Christian brother or a friend
- **Ex-Boyfriend/Girlfriend**: Past commitment that there is no longer an attachment to.

CHAPTER 16

Locations in Dreams

The location or scenery in which a dream takes place can help you accurately discern what aspect of your life the dream is talking about. For example, a dream where you see yourself in **school** may pertain to being in a season of learning and equipping or needing to unlearn some things as a prerequisite to moving forward.

A dream where you see yourself in a **hospital** may have something to do with healing. It may be physical healing, inner healing, or spiritual healing.

A dream in your **grandparent's home** may pertain to inheritance. That is, something generational that runs in the bloodline, and it may either be a blessing or a curse.

Some Common Symbolic Locations

- **House**: A person (owner of the house) or a dwelling place.

Luke 11:24 *When an unclean spirit goes out of a **man**, he goes through dry places, seeking rest; and finding none, he says, 'I will return to my **house** from which I came.'*

- **Childhood home**: The past

This helps to pinpoint when the issue at hand took root. It provides both an age range and a location.

> **Key Point:** A lot of things we experience today are the result of seeds sown at different points in our lives.

- **Grandparents' home**: Inheritance (Blessing or Curse)

Seeing your paternal or maternal grandparents lets you know from which side of your family the "inheritance" in question originated from.

Key Point: Particular attention should be paid to dreams that contain grandparents, as they usually pertain to some kind of inheritance.

The same way a house represents a person, different areas of the house can sometimes represent different aspects or areas of a person's life.

- **Living Room**: A present-day problem, a current affair, a revelation, or the truth exposed. The living room is usually symbolically signifying that the dream is about something the dreamer is currently facing.
- **Kitchen**: the heart, intent, motives, plans, or ambition. Primarily, the kitchen represents the heart.
- **Bathroom**: Cleansing, prayer of repentance, confession of offenses or sins to another person. The state of the toilet or bathroom and the dreamer's ability or inability to use them provide a strong pointer to the ability of the dreamer to fully repent as needed, or if there is a hindrance stopping the dreamer from fully repenting.
- **Bedroom**: rest, intimacy, privacy, covenant (marriage). Watch out for a cluttered **bed,** as your intimacy (with God or your Spouse) or your rest is being hindered.

- **Basement**: carnal nature, lust, discouragement or depression, refuge, being hidden, or secret sin.
- **Back yard or back door:** The past, previous event or experience (good or evil), something behind in time, such as your past sins or forefathers' sins, unaware, unsuspecting, or hidden.

As always, it is very important to emphasize that understanding the context of a dream is integral to our ability to properly apply meanings to the symbols used therein.

Directions in Dreams

*Genesis 12:10 Now there was a famine in the land, and Abram **went down** to **Egypt** to dwell there, for the famine was severe in the land.*

*Genesis 26:2 Then the Lord appeared to him and said, "Do not **go down** to **Egypt**; live in the land of which I shall tell you.*

*Isaiah 31:1 Woe to those who **go down** to **Egypt** for help and rely on horses, who trust in chariots because they are many.*

*Genesis 46:3-4 So He said, "I am God, the God of your father; do not fear to **go down** to **Egypt**, for I will make of you a great nation there.*

Genesis 13:1 *Then Abram **went up** from **Egypt**, he and his wife and all that he had, and Lot with him, to the south.*

Left or Right?

As with most symbols, the symbolic meaning of **left** and **right** in a dream is dependent on the context in which they are used. As a general principle, whenever you have a choice between turning left or right in a dream, the right direction is *almost* always the correct choice.

My ex-colleague, who is Muslim, shared a dream he had with me where he found himself in the middle. On the left was a mosque, and on the right was a person. He recognized the person as Jesus Christ. Then, he woke up.

The interpretation of the dream is simple: **Jesus is the right way.**

Someone else shared a dream with me where two people went in different directions. One went right, and the other person went left. The person who went right was on his way to a church fellowship and encountered Jesus on his way, while the person who went left was trying to bring order to a chaotic environment with little success.

In this dream, the left turn represents works of the flesh, and the right turn represents dependence on God and His grace. The interpretation is, therefore, that **fellowship with Jesus is the key.**

Left-handed Warriors

Have you ever wondered about this scripture?

Judges 20:16 *Out of all these people were seven hundred choice left-handed men; each one could sling stones at [a target no wider than] a hair and not miss.*

Why did they find it necessary to include the fact that they were left-handed?

It was included to indicate to us that their exploits were empowered by The Holy Spirit. The **left hand** oftentimes represents what we are **spiritually empowered** to do, and our **right hand** represents what we are **naturally endowed** to do.

CHAPTER 17

Vehicles in Dreams

In a dream, you may see yourself in a certain kind of vehicle and wonder if that holds any importance in the interpretation of the dream. In this chapter, we will look at some vehicles and their possible interpretations.

1. Car

A car generally represents a person's **life**. Depending on the context of the dream, we can deduce the specific area it refers to, such as **ministry, career or marriage**, amongst other fields. A car is a means of transportation from one location to another and could show progress.

There are several types of cars.

What kind of car do you see yourself in? A sports car, a regular sedan or a car that looks like it fits in the Fred-Flintstone era?

Below is a list of different kinds of cars and what they represent:

- School bus: Teaching ministry.
- Sports car: Speed.
- Station wagon: Family.
- Convertible with top up: Having a covering. Adequately covered.

- Convertible with top down: being uncovered, having everything revealed, open, nothing hidden, and exposed to attack.
- Jeep or four-wheel drive: Full-time ministry or being equipped to successfully navigate areas others may not be able to.

In addition to the type of car you see yourself in, it is important to pay attention to your position inside the car. Are you driving? Are you a passenger sitting in the front passenger seat or sitting in the back seat?

The position you occupy in the car gives an idea of how much control the dreamer has over the situation in which he or she is being depicted.

- **Driving a car:** represents being in control of the situation or determining the direction of the situation.
- **Passenger front seat (co-pilot):** not necessarily in control but positioned to **influence** the direction of the situation.
- **Passenger back seat**: very limited influence on the outcome of the situation. Other people's decisions will have an impact on the dreamer (positively or negatively), and the dreamer cannot change it. It may also mean that the dreamer may have delegated his responsibilities to someone else and finds himself in a position where he can no longer exert the control he should normally have.

Cars can also be used as a negative symbol in a dream. The most common form of this is when a car is parked in such a way that the dreamer's vehicle cannot move. This represents a **hindrance**. The more cars are parked, the greater the hindrance.

Symbols and symbolic actions frequently employ the physical world to reveal hidden meanings to the dreamer. Because of this, we can usually determine the seriousness of a dream's message by comparing it to the same circumstance in real life.

As mentioned earlier, a car often symbolizes a person's life. By considering the context of the dream, we can determine the particular aspect it is referring to, be it ministry, career, marriage, or other areas.

The car may experience certain events that symbolically convey a message to the dreamer about their current state or condition on their journey.

A dream of an **automobile crash involving another car** (fender bender) is a warning that the dreamer will be involved in an altercation, argument, or dispute with another person.

An **auto-wreck all by yourself** represents a warning of a mistake or sin that will affect the particular area the car represents in the dream.

Tires represent a person's spirit, and the state of the tires gives a clue to the person's spiritual condition. A **deflated tire** may represent discouragement or dismay.

Ezekiel 1:20 *Wherever the spirit wanted to go, they went, because there the spirit went; and the wheels were lifted together with them, for the spirit of the living creatures was in the wheels.*

A **deflated tire** may also represent a hindrance because a car cannot move with a flat tire, at least not as fast as it would normally move.

The context of the dream is always crucial in understanding the meaning of a symbol. If the tires are worn out as a result of negligence or lack of proper maintenance that points to a lack of prayer, which leads to discouragement and dismay on the journey. If someone, however, tampered with the car, it represents a hindrance.

Key Point: It is always important to remember that almost every symbol has a wide variety of meanings, both positive and negative. To accurately know which meaning to ascribe to the symbol shown in your dream, carefully consider the context in which the symbol was shown.

Properly functioning brakes in a car are required to enable the driver to slow down or stop when required. In a general context, **brakes** represent the ability to stop. Depending on the context, it also represents a call to wait or even a hindrance.If the **brakes fail** in a car, the driver loses the ability to determine his speed or the direction in which he is going. As such**, failed brakes** or an inability to stop represents a lack of control, an inability to resist temptation, or an inability to discontinue a bad habit or change. On the flipside, an inability to use the brakes could also be a call for the dreamer to give up trying to chart their course in life and trust the Holy Spirit to lead. This is especially true for people who are stubborn or strong-willed and are prone to self-reliance. They typically do not wait for or seek God's opinion.

One of the most important components in any car is the **engine.** In its simplest definition, an engine is a machine with moving parts that converts power into motion. The keyword there is *motion,* as it empowers the car to move forward, which signifies progress.

Any dream that contains or references a car's engine should be taken with all seriousness, especially if it contains someone trying to tamper with or remove the engine. It is a call for serious prayers.

2. Airplanes

Airplanes soar through the **air** and are one of the fastest means of transportation. A lot of times, an airplane is used to depict something that is empowered by the Holy Spirit (air).

The first thing to pay attention to is what type or size of airplane you find yourself in. The bigger the plane, the larger the impact.

A **jumbo jet** is representative of a large corporation or ministry.

A **fighter jet** is representative of a personal warfare ministry. It is personal because most fighter jets are one-seaters.

A **passenger jet** represents a church or career.

A **small airplane** represents a person or personal ministry.

3. Train

Trains move on a predetermined path that cannot be altered. The path of the train is determined by the railroad tracks.

A train is used to symbolize the church or something that is continuous or unchanging, for instance, God's Word which is the same forever.

Railroad tracks symbolize tradition. Trains usually have stops where passengers embark and disembark from the train. Likewise, in a dream, this may be representative of a temporary or seasonal endeavor for the dreamer.

4. Bicycle

A bicycle represents a personal ministry or endeavor that has a lot of "works". Such a person is not dependent on faith.

CHAPTER 18

You Are Already Blessed With All Spiritual Blessings

Ephesians 1:3

*Blessed be the God and Father of our Lord Jesus Christ, who **has** **blessed** us with every spiritual blessing in heavenly places in Christ.*

"Has blessed" in that verse is in the past tense, connoting that it has already been done!

One day, as I was pondering this verse and why I still had not seen the manifestation of some gifts and abilities that I had been praying for, God reminded me of when I used to play video games as a child. I developed a habit of diligently completing video games, ensuring that I conquered every level and emerged victorious by defeating the final "bad guy".

There were some challenging games with exceptionally difficult levels and bosses that proved to be extremely tough to overcome. At times, the challenges were so formidable that I would find myself stuck for an extended period of time, tirelessly searching for a solution to overcome them. I persevered through numerous failures, refusing to give up until I ultimately triumphed over the level or boss.

I always finished every game I played.

God showed me that the reason I always continued to try to beat those levels was because I had an **unwavering inner belief** that there was no game I could not win.

> **Key Point**: The unwavering belief in my own inherent ability served as a powerful motivation, often compelling me to persist even when everything looked like I should give up.

To consistently see the manifestation of any spiritual gift, I believe that this same inner belief must be present. You must believe, without doubt, that the ability to access and manifest the gift has already been deposited in you. This is what the scripture means when it says, **"He has *already* blessed us with every spiritual blessing."**

For dream interpretation, I have learned to trust The Holy Spirit to help make dreams clear to me. No matter how complex or strange a dream is, I don't put any pressure on myself because I am not the one to unravel it; the Holy Spirit will unravel it for me and help me to understand.

This is highly important because people sometimes look to a person as the source of assistance, but I know that I am not, and it removes from me every form of pressure or need to "perform".

In spite of what I have just described above, it still requires that I spend time pondering and studying a dream, sometimes even hours looking at it until light breaks forth and my understanding is fruitful. The push to keep trying to understand even after sitting for hours stems from an inner belief that the gift is active in my life, and if I wait on God, He will eventually reveal the meaning to me.

You can enjoy the same thing because **you** have already been blessed with all spiritual blessings.

Key Point: Our inner belief produces our exhibited behavior.

It All Starts With Your Faith: Do You Believe?

When someone is telling me about their dream, I automatically listen with the full intention of understanding and interpreting the hidden message in the dream. Though the dream may sound long, have so many strange elements in it, and be the most confusing thing I have ever heard in my life, deep down on the inside of me, I know that I can understand the meaning of the dream.

It all starts with belief.

I can do this because I firmly believe that it is not me but the Holy Spirit who empowers my mind to understand. My faith drives me to seek even greater experiences and insights from Him.

Your faith is the bedrock of operating in any gift of the Spirit. You must believe. Settle it in your heart that there is nothing the Holy Spirit cannot teach you. Your belief will manifest in your attitude and will ultimately determine your actions and the fruit you see.

Looking back at the process God has taken me through on my journey of interpreting dreams, I have realized that He blessed me with a nurturing environment where my faith in His ability to help me understand my dreams was nurtured and cultivated.

In the beginning, Pastor Alex interpreted a lot of my dreams, and I had the opportunity to observe the process. For him, it appeared to be very easy.

He always displayed simple faith.

"Father, this is what was shown to your son; what does it mean?" He would ask. The Holy Spirit would quicken his understanding, and he would give the interpretation. It looked all so simple.

When I started attempting to interpret my dreams, it didn't quite work like that. I would sit down, pray, and reflect on the dream, trying to figure it out without making any headway.

God led me to John Paul Jackson, and I watched his teachings on dreams and his live dream interpretation sessions over and over again. He also led me to read some books on biblical dream interpretation and the meaning of symbols in dreams.

> **Key Lesson**: Sometimes, answers to your prayer are in a book or a conversation with someone that you just "happen" to come across. We must always remain sensitive.

I share this with you today because I want you to truly believe that **you can do it.** Your belief is the starting point. Ask Him and trust Him to help you, then start acting out your faith!

There are some people who are blessed with the uncommon gift of being able to understand mysteries without prior knowledge, exposure, or study of the subject. These people are few and far between. For the majority of us, the scripture below holds the key.

2 Tim 2: 15 *Study to show thyself approved unto God.*

I will share a little story from my journey to understanding my dreams and the lessons I learned from the experience.

At that time, I had seen a certain amount of improvement in my ability to understand and interpret dreams, both mine and the dreams of others. Sometimes it would come easy and other times it would be so difficult that I would doubt myself and question if God had really equipped me to do this.

One day, I had this vivid dream that I knew had a great meaning but despite several attempts to understand it, the interpretation eluded me. I had previously come across a biblical dream interpreter, read some of her articles, and respected her as someone truly gifted in the ability to understand dreams.

One night, while searching for answers to understand a particular dream, I came across her website and saw that there was an offer to pay for your dreams to be interpreted. The process seemed pretty simple and straightforward. Pay the specified amount of money, send her your dream, she will interpret it, and send the interpretation back to you.

I was in luck! It seemed like God had finally answered my prayers.

So, I whipped out my bank card, punched in the details, and paid the requested fee. I also needed to register with my email address. After pressing the authorization for the payment to be processed, I got an email. It was a payment receipt and an e-book for me. I never got the link to the portal through which I would have submitted my dream. Instead of a portal to submit the dream, I got a book.

Then I understood what God was saying.

Shortcuts and reliance on a person are not the way. I needed to keep studying, praying, learning, and expanding my own knowledge. God knew that if I had submitted that dream to her and she had responded with an accurate interpretation that would be the end of my own pursuit. I would have had my own dream interpreter and probably never really pressed into Him for understanding.

God's word to you is, "Study to show yourself approved unto God."

There are no shortcuts to achieving real success in the things of God. There is always a price to pay. We either determine to roll our sleeves up and dig in deep, with a clear conviction that He will reward our efforts, or we remain at the surface level and miss out on what He really has for us.

It is your choice to make, and I earnestly urge you to choose wisely.

BONUS CHAPTER

Your Obedience Unlocks the Door: My Journey to Marriage

On the **20th of January, 2013**, I had a dream:

In the dream, I am sitting at a table with three other people—two women and a man. A song came on about a man apologizing to a woman for breaking her heart and asking for her forgiveness. One of the women on the table started to cry to the song, like it was being sung directly to her. When it was over, she had tears in her eyes, and her makeup was smudged a little bit. She then became defensive and asked about my age. She said that I must be no more than 19. I responded, telling her that I was 22. The other man on the table was also seemingly young. I did not recognize anyone at the table, and the dream ended suddenly.

Pay special attention to the dreams you receive at the beginning of the year. I have found that they tend to provide insightful information and direction for the things required to possess the promises God has for you within the year.

When I woke up from this dream, I was not sure what it meant, but I wrote it down and pondered it in my heart. In the past, I had been in a deliberately undefined relationship with a particular lady that did not end well, and I knew she was heartbroken at the time. I had justified my decision at the time, but in my heart, I knew that this dream was asking me to make amends by apologizing. Although I

137

had an idea of what I was meant to do, I hesitated, partly because I did not have a full understanding of the dream and also because a part of me still believed that my actions at the time were justified.

Fast- forward to August of the same year and, I bought and read Understanding the Dreams You Dream Volume 2 by Ira Milligan. As I was reading the book, I went back to my dream journal to start looking through all my dreams that had numbers in them. When I came upon this dream, I had greater clarity on the meaning of the numbers 19 and 22.

The Interpretation

I need to apologize to the girl whose heart was broken for release from this.

Nineteen (19) - Lack of fruit or harvest, Barren

Twenty-Two (22):

Twenty - Holy (separated unto God and accepted by Him)

Two - To set apart

There were four people sitting at the table, me and three other people.

The song that came on with the man apologizing to the woman and asking for forgiveness was an instruction for me.

The woman crying as soon as the song came on represented the fact that the pain was still there. Then she addressed me directly in a confrontational way, like she was taking it out on me. This revealed that I was the cause of her tears and the subject of the dream.

When I had this dream, I was 28 years old. This immediately revealed that the numbers 19 and 22 were symbolic. By saying that I was no more than **19**, she was speaking of a lack of harvest. Within the context of relationships, this means fruitless relationships – relationships that will not lead to marriage. I responded by stating that I was 22 years old, which served as a reaffirmation of my identity in Christ.

It is important to note that despite my position in Christ, as highlighted by my affirmation, the instruction to apologize was not invalidated. In fact, it was my position in Christ, as a child of God that compelled me to apologize.

As soon as I understood what the full message of the dream was, I knew that I had to make things right.

Although the dream and instruction remained at the forefront of my mind, I was hesitant to follow through with it and made different excuses in my mind: I did not have her number, I did not have her email address, and I was not even sure where in the world she was.

In October of that same year, I finally searched for her online, connected with her, and asked for her Skype ID. She gave it to me, and I called her. She was surprised by my call, and when I apologized to her about the way things happened, she accepted my apology and asked if I was now "born again," to which I responded, yes.

I had obeyed the instruction.

I would like to provide some background information. During that particular phase of my life, I had firmly decided to actively seek and pursue God's will in every aspect of my life, including marriage.

I first met Esther in December 2012 at a Christmas party hosted by a friend, and we remained friends, communicating mostly via WhatsApp chat.

On the same day, I obeyed the instruction God had given me to apologize, my relationship with Esther transitioned from a simple friendship to recognizing that there was something potentially there.

We both acknowledge without any doubt in our minds that our conversation that day ushered in a new era in our "friendship".

We got married a year and a half later. The impact of my obedience was not evident at first; it was a couple of years later, while looking back at the events, that it became clear that both seemingly unconnected events took place on the same day.

Coincidence? I believe not.

I believe that God orchestrated it this way to help me see very clearly the link between my obedience and my breakthrough.

It is also important to note that I met Esther in December 2012 and had this dream in January 2013. Obedience to the instruction in the dream unlocked the door to the possibility of marriage with Esther.

Is it possible that you are asking God for something that He has already provided the answer to, but the prayer continues because there is a lack of understanding?

Our obedience is not for God's benefit; it is always for ours, even though it seldom looks or seems like it at first.

Treasure God's instructions and act on them promptly.

God's love is limitless, and He seeks to show you just how much He loves you, even through the dreams He gives you. Embrace His love for you, and make up your mind to obey His every instruction.

I am rooting for you!

Bibliography

1. Milligan, Ira, and Judy Milligan. *Understanding the Dreams You Dream: Biblical Keys for Hearing God's Voice in the Night.* 1997.

2. Milligan, Ira L. *Understanding the Dreams You Dream, Vol. 2.* 2006. *Bowker*, https://doi.org/10.1604/9781424503100.

3. Pax-Harry, Obii. *Prophetic Engagement: The Issachar Mandate.* 2006. *Bowker*, https://doi.org/10.1604/9788889127315.

4. Ibojie, Joe. *Illustrated Dictionary of Dream Symbols: A Biblical Guide to Your Dreams and Visions.* 2010.

5. Hagin, Kenneth E. *The Believer's Authority.* 1985. *Bowker*, https://doi.org/10.1604/9780892764068.

6. Thompson, Adam, and Adrian Beale. *The Divinity Code to Understanding Your Dreams and Visions.* 2011.

7. Milligan, Ira, and Judy Milligan. *Understanding the Dreams You Dream: Biblical Keys for Hearing God's Voice in the Night.* 1997.

8. S. Wong, B. C. (2016, January 5). *The Dream Interpreter.*

9. Goll, James W. *The Seer: The Prophetic Power of Visions, Dreams, and Open Heavens.* 2005. *Bowker*, https://doi.org/10.1604/9780768422320.

ABOUT THE AUTHOR

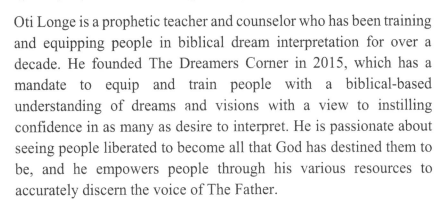

Oti Longe is a prophetic teacher and counselor who has been training and equipping people in biblical dream interpretation for over a decade. He founded The Dreamers Corner in 2015, which has a mandate to equip and train people with a biblical-based understanding of dreams and visions with a view to instilling confidence in as many as desire to interpret. He is passionate about seeing people liberated to become all that God has destined them to be, and he empowers people through his various resources to accurately discern the voice of The Father.

Oti is joyfully married to Esther and they have two wonderful children.

For more information about Oti Longe, outreaches, ministry, media and other materials, please visit:

Website: *www.otilonge.com*

Instagram: **www.instagram.com** **/the_dreamerscorner**

YouTube: **www.youtube.com** **/@thedreamerscorner**

Contact Oti Longe:

info@otilonge.com

Printed in Poland
by Amazon Fulfillment
Poland Sp. z o.o., Wrocław

30220144R00088